make
your
dreams

simple steps for changing the beliefs that limit you

come

Pamala Oslie

true

AMBER-ALLEN PUBLISHING

SAN RAFAEL, CALIFORNIA

Copyright © 1998 by Pamala Oslie

Published by Amber-Allen Publishing, Inc.
Post Office Box 6657
San Rafael, California 94903

Editorial: Janet Mills
Cover Design: Michele Wetherbee / doubleugee
Cover Photograph: Photonica, ETC
Typography: Rick Gordon, Emerald Valley Graphics

Library of Congress Cataloging-in-Publication Data

Oslie, Pamala, 1952–
    Make your dreams come true : simple steps for changing the beliefs
    that limit you / by Pamala Oslie.
        p.   cm.
    ISBN 1-878424-33-5 (alk. paper)
    1. Belief and doubt.   2. Change (Psychology)   3. Self-
actualization (Psychology)   I. Title.
    BF773.065   1998   98–15626
    158.1 — dc21   CIP

ISBN 1-878424-33-5

Printed in Canada on acid-free paper
Distributed by Publishers Group West
10 9 8 7 6 5 4 3 2 1

This book is dedicated to the loving and
adventurous souls that we are.

Love, joy, and fulfillment to all . . . .

To Thanya,
Believe
+ go for it!
Pamala Oracle

contents

introduction   1

part one: The Power of Belief   7

   one: your true creative power   9

   two: the facts or the truth?   19

part two: Discovering Your Beliefs   29

   three: the origin of beliefs   31

   four: games and processes   45

part three: Changing Your Beliefs   81

   five: methods for changing your beliefs   83

   six: a look at limiting beliefs   113

part four: Creating with New Beliefs   143

   seven: living the life of your dreams   145

   eight: the shortcut to happiness and fulfillment   157

about the author   165

acknowledgments

I wish to express my gratitude and appreciation to my family and my extended family of friends. I hope you all know how much you mean to me and how deeply I love you. Part of who I am is because of you and your love and support of me. Mere words could not express how much I value each of you. I am so glad that we have chosen to share this adventure together; it wouldn't have been nearly as much fun without you! Thank you again for being who you are. I love you now and always from the depths of my heart.

introduction

Like so many people I know, I have spent my life searching for "the truth." I wanted to find the answers to life's most important questions: Who are we? Who or what is God? What is life all about? How can I find and experience true love? Can I really attain total fulfillment and happiness in this lifetime? Is it possible to have everything my heart desires? Deep down I believed the answers were attainable; I also believed they would be simple and yet profound.

Although I found myself caught up in the daily activities of working, doing household chores, and attempting to create a meaningful relationship, I never abandoned my search for the answers to life's deeper mysteries. I delved into countless theories and ideas about love, life, God, who we are, and how we fit into the entire scheme of things. I studied the words of great philosophers, spiritual teachers, dedicated scientists, physicists, physicians, and others considered to be "authorities" from around the world.

Western scientists, biologists, and physicians taught me that I was a physical organism with purely biological capabilities. From science I learned that my brain controls the functions of my body, my personality, and my thought processes; and that in time, I would grow old, die, and cease to exist.

My religion taught me that while I had a physical body that would someday return to the dust of the earth, I also had a soul. One day this soul would either spend eternity in heaven at the feet of God or burn eternally in the fires of hell. My fate depended entirely on whether I was a good girl or a bad girl, and whether I believed and accepted what that religion taught me.

Society taught me that I needed to have a certain appearance to be liked and accepted by others. I needed to work in socially acceptable jobs to be valuable and to fit in. Society also taught me that I should be married by a certain age or I would be considered odd or an "old maid."

Each time society tried to force me inside strict boundaries, to match its definition of what is normal and acceptable, my immediate reaction was to rebel. Something deep within me cried out for freedom, as if I intuitively knew there was a boundless, creative power inside us, waiting to be recognized. This inner knowing, and my natural desire to have a more expansive, empowering experience of life, drove me to find higher answers.

What I discovered dramatically changed my life. I discovered that we are profoundly more powerful and creative than I had ever been taught to believe! We are boundless, unlimited beings; we are masters of our own destinies. There is something magical and mysterious about who we are, something grand and magnificent: We create our own experiences through the power of our thoughts, feelings, and beliefs. Our ability to create what we want is limited only by our imagination and by the belief that we are limited. Too often we are taught to believe that our experience of life is the way life is, so we don't even consider that our experience is just one version of what life is or what it *could* be if we opened our mind to other possibilities.

As I began to practice the theories and methods that I discovered, I began to connect with my true inner power. My life was completely transformed; it became easier, more fulfilling, and much more fun. Although I don't always put all the principles I learned into practice, I am always *aware* of them, and my life continues to improve each day. Because I understand that my thoughts, feelings, and beliefs create my experiences, I can choose to create a loving relationship, a continuous flow of abundance, freedom to travel, my own successful business, a beautiful home in the location of my dreams, great friends, excellent health — basically everything I have always wanted.

The principles I choose to live by now include the following:

1) We are powerful beings with no limits to what we can create. We have an inherent ability to create our experience through the power of our beliefs, thoughts, and feelings.

2) We have free will. We can choose our beliefs and change our reality; we can create whatever we desire.

3) We limit our ability to create what we desire by limiting our perceptions of what is possible. If we repeatedly affirm our belief in limitations, we will continue to experience them. As we begin to affirm that we are unlimited, we begin to perceive and experience new freedoms.

Everything in our lives originates within us. We create or draw to us every experience and person that exists in our lives. This idea can frighten or upset us until we discover the real freedom and power that lies within it. By knowing that we are the creators of our experience, we also come to realize that we can change our experience if we aren't happy with our creations.

I believe life is a creative adventure and there are no right or wrong ways to live. I support your choice to believe whatever you want to believe. I also believe we make life tougher on ourselves when we accept self-limiting, self-defeating, self-critical beliefs.

This book is designed to help you get in touch with your beliefs and discover how those beliefs are affecting your life. You will find various games and processes designed to reveal your beliefs. The origin of your beliefs will also be revealed, and you will learn methods for discarding useless, self-limiting, and fear-based beliefs that are responsible for creating unpleasant situations and circumstances in your life.

You can create the life of your dreams. It is my sincere desire to help you gain insights into the profound process of creation so that you can create a magical, joyful, and fulfilling life.

part one

The Power of Belief

"You cannot see the wind directly — you see only its effects. The same applies to your thoughts. They possess power as the wind does, but you only see the effects of their actions."

—"SETH," JANE ROBERTS, *The Way Toward Health*

one

your true creative power

Most people never stop to question what they have been taught about life. It may not occur to us that our thoughts and beliefs about life are just that: *beliefs* about life and not necessarily *the truth*. We may never examine or challenge these beliefs because we are so accustomed to what our lives have become that we don't look beyond our current perceptions. We accept what we have been taught as the one and only reality.

All too often we live our lives feeling trapped or stuck with unpleasant situations. We live with all kinds of circumstances that we wish we could change, but we don't believe that we can or ever will change them. We tend to believe, despite our deepest longings and desires, that these are our only possible choices, that this is just the way life is.

There is a powerful and creative force within each of us. This creative power flows through us and around us, forming everything in the world, both visible and invisible. This force is also responsible for manifesting our desires. Our thoughts and beliefs convey images to this inner force, and interesting coincidences begin to happen; events occur with amazing synchronicity to bring our inner images into physical form. Whatever energy we send out into the world comes back to us. As we believe, we create.

When we hold onto limiting thoughts and beliefs, we limit what is truly available to us through this creative force. We also hinder the natural, spontaneous magic of this force by failing to be aware of our connection to it. Life then becomes a struggle instead of a magical experience.

We can learn how to fully actualize our potential and live with the awareness of this inner power. Of course, we can also choose to ignore this power or to believe that it doesn't exist. Whether we use this power consciously or unconsciously, we are still responsible for creating our experience. Since our life reflects our beliefs, if our beliefs are limiting and fear-based, we will have limiting and fearful experiences.

We may not even be aware that we have certain beliefs. Imagine a glass of water with sediment in the bottom of the glass. Looking at the water, it appears to be clear. However, when you taste the water, it is bitter and metallic. If you stir up the water, the sediment rises, and you can see the impurities that are giving the water a bad taste. Once you can see what is causing the problem, you can choose to clean out the impurities and have pleasant-tasting water instead. Looking at your life, are you ready to stir up the "sediments," or limiting beliefs, that have caused you to create less-than-pleasant experiences in your life?

Let's begin by considering the following questions:

Do you believe that you have little or no control over your destiny, or do you believe you have complete dominion over your own life?

Do you often feel you are a victim of circumstances, society, or other people, or do you believe that you have free will and creative choices in your life?

Do you see how you are responsible for creating your life experiences, or do you believe that forces beyond your control are responsible for your life experiences?

Some people believe they can heal their own bodies. Others believe they are at the mercy of diseases, germs, and bacteria, with little or no defense against the attack of these organisms.

Some people believe they can easily generate wealth and live in abundance. Others believe they are destined to be poor, or to live as helpless victims in a jobless society.

Some people believe it is easy to meet someone and fall in love. Others believe they have no control over whether they will ever have love in their lives.

The difference in people's experiences lies in their beliefs about life. How much creative power do you believe you have? Look at the line below and mark the place that best describes how much power you believe you have to create the life you choose.

I have 0 percent
creative power

I have 100 percent
creative power

Do you believe that you create some of the events

and experiences in your life, but not all of them? If so, where do you draw the line and why do you draw it there? *due to others' free will*

Where we draw the line between having no creative power or having unlimited creative power depends upon our beliefs about reality in general and how safe we feel with the concept of being powerful. Most people fall somewhere in between the two extremes.

I believe we have 100 percent creative power and that we limit our power because we are afraid of it. We deny our real capabilities because we don't trust ourselves. We have been led to believe that we are capable of abusing power or of making mistakes. That belief is often based on another belief that we are inherently bad, weak, stupid, or sinful. Because we mistrust ourselves, we limit our ability to create the lives we dream of. In addition, because we believe that we are somehow inadequate, we often live with stress and constant worry about what may happen tomorrow because we are not smart enough or capable enough to prepare for it today. When we let go of our critical self-judgments, when we learn to trust ourselves and our inner voice, we will no longer hold back our true power.

The Power to Choose

Any idea that you accept as truth is a belief. Your beliefs prompt your actions, expectations, and emotions, which then create your experiences. Thoughts that are repeated and reinforced each day become the basis for the repetitive behavior that creates the same results — again and again.

Your life is a living picture of your beliefs. You won't always get what you desire, but you will always get what you believe. If you want to know what you believe, take an objective look at your life. If you have a life filled with happiness, health, and love, your beliefs are working for you. If your life is filled with frustration, depression, lack, or struggle, your beliefs are working against you.

It is time for us to move beyond "victim consciousness" and take responsibility for our own lives. It is time that we realize we are not at the mercy of events that happen to us. This is not to be unsympathetic or harsh toward people who suffer hardships, but to empower them to see that if they have problems in their lives, they can also create love, peace, health, abundance, and harmony just as easily.

When we suffer from hardships and challenges, we

don't need to criticize ourselves for the life we have created. We simply need to acknowledge our part in creating these conditions and then choose to create something better. The more we become aware of our creative abilities, the more we will know that our choices are unlimited. If we are not aware of our creative power, it will appear as though we have no choices. It will seem as though we are at the mercy of circumstances beyond our control.

We have the power to choose what we will think about and therefore what we will create. We can choose to think about our problems and our fears, or we can choose to think about our joys and our blessings. We can choose to think about reasons to be happy, or we can choose to think about reasons to be unhappy. We also assign value and significance to different events and circumstances. We decide what will make us happy, sad, angry, or fulfilled. If we have a belief that certain events and situations will make us happy, then when those situations occur, we will experience feelings of happiness.

Some people believe that marriage provides a sense of security, which makes them happy. Others see marriage as a prison, which makes them unhappy. Some people believe children provide joy, warmth, and comfort, which makes them happy. Others consider children a burdensome responsibility, which makes them unhappy. Some people believe life should be full of adventure and excitement; they want to challenge life and explore new horizons. Others prefer a life of solitude and quiet reflection; they want a safe, secure, and comfortable existence. Everyone has a unique life experience because no two people have the same beliefs, desires, or perspectives.

If you take the time to examine your thoughts and beliefs, you are likely to discover certain ideas that limit and hinder you. You can learn to let go of critical, fearful, self-judgmental thoughts. You can learn to trust yourself and your own inner voice. When you clear out the negative, self-limiting judgments, you free yourself to express your true creative power.

Before you can change your limiting beliefs, you must first become aware of what they are. Start by listening to your inner dialogue. What repetitive thoughts are going through your mind? Are they fearsome, worried, and pessimistic, or are they joyful, optimistic, and enthusiastic? If you pay attention to your thoughts, you can discover your beliefs. There are no deep, dark inaccessible thoughts that are locked away forever in your subconscious. You have access to every aspect of your mind if you will simply be still and listen.

Your emotions are another important clue to your beliefs because your emotions always follow your thoughts. If you are experiencing feelings of anxiety, worry, hopelessness, or depression, this is the first clue that a limiting belief is causing trouble. If you are sad or depressed, ask yourself what you have been thinking about or dwelling upon. Then ask yourself what beliefs might be responsible for generating these unhappy thoughts.

Most of us allow the same habitual thoughts to wander aimlessly in and out of our mind. We have millions of thoughts every day, but most of them are identical to the thoughts we had yesterday. You can become aware of what you think and choose your thoughts consciously, or you can allow your mind and emotions to run wild and create unpleasant circum-stances in your life. By consciously choosing your thoughts and beliefs, you become a conscious creator of your life. You become the master of your creations.

two

the facts or the truth?

We have based most of our beliefs about life on "the facts" given to us by others. But can we trust "the facts" to give us an accurate version of reality? It used to be considered a fact that the earth was flat. It was also considered a fact that the earth was stationary and that the sun and other planets revolved around the earth. These widespread mass beliefs profoundly affected the way people perceived the universe and their place within it.

Eventually, when it was discovered that the earth was round and revolved around the sun, this discovery affected many other beliefs and "facts." What was once seen as a fact was no longer accepted as true. There was a shift in perception, and with that shift came a new world of opportunities, possibilities, and freedom.

We have been taught that we are limited, physical beings who must live within certain "realistic" boundaries. But can we trust science or any generally accepted "facts" to give us a true picture of who we are? Science, religion, medicine, and other disciplines have always provided us with "the facts" as if they were the one and only truth. The problem is that "the facts" and "the truth" according to these disciplines are always changing.

Western science, for example, provides us with countless "facts" about the limitations of the human body. It tells us that our body is only capable of certain things. However, extraordinary feats of human skill and endurance, once considered beyond our physical capabilities, occur every day. People are running faster, jumping higher, and lifting more weight than was ever believed possible. World records in sports and other human endeavors are being broken and surpassed all the time. What are the true limitations of the human body?

There are many reports of people who perform "impossible" feats. One such account tells of a woman who was able to lift a car off her husband after the jack shifted and the car fell on top of him. Who would have imagined this was possible? How often do we surpass the preconceived notions of what is possible in our own lives? There are numerous people who spontaneously heal themselves of so-called "terminal" illnesses and go on to live long, healthy lives. We have been told that to heal ourselves of certain diseases is physically impossible. By what standards do we judge what is possible or impossible?

We didn't know there were microscopic creatures until the invention of the microscope. We were not aware of certain stars and planets in space until the invention of the telescope. We didn't believe we could fly until we discovered the principles of aerodynamics. What else don't we know because we haven't understood certain principles or discovered more "facts"? What don't we know about ourselves because we have not yet created the technology to reveal this information? What don't we currently understand because we have not allowed our consciousness to expand, to dream, or to imagine the possibilities beyond what science, psychology, medicine, or religion have taught us?

The Turtle and the Frog

There was once a turtle who surfaced from his home in the ocean and walked across the land to a nearby pond. At the pond, he encountered a frog sitting on a lily pad. The frog asked the turtle who he was and where he came from. The turtle responded that he had come from the great ocean. Having never heard of the ocean, the frog asked the turtle to explain what the ocean was and how big it was. Was it as big as his lily pad? "Much bigger," the turtle responded. Was it as big as the large rock in the center of the pond? "Much bigger," the turtle answered. The turtle explained to the frog that the ocean was a great body of water and was hundreds of times greater than the size of the pond. The frog became angry and yelled at the turtle, "You are an impostor and a liar! There is nothing bigger or greater than this pond. I have lived in this pond my entire life. I have covered every inch of this pond, and I know that there cannot be anything bigger than this pond!" And with that the frog turned his back on the turtle and swam away.

We may no longer want to live like the frog and rely on "the facts" to provide us with an accurate description of human potential. All too often we close our minds to so many things that we have not yet experienced, that we do not understand, or that cannot be proven by the "experts."

Each of us, at one time or another, has probably experienced fear and resistance to change. Change can frighten us. We feel safer and more secure within our protective and familiar boundaries. New ideas often create fear, mistrust, chaos, and confusion. When Galileo announced that the earth revolved around the sun, people thought the statement was blasphemous, and they imprisoned him. The information threatened the belief system of the times and threw people's known and familiar structures into chaos and disorder.

The pace of change has accelerated dramatically in our lifetime. It is challenging enough to keep up with all the changes in our personal lives, let alone the changes in technology and the global consciousness. We are in the process of learning new concepts and expanding our ideas about the world we live in.

As we move into an expanded level of awareness, one of the challenges we will experience involves a new understanding of who we really are and what we are capable of doing. We are discovering that we are far more than physical machines that are limited by our circumstances and environment.

There are so many things that cannot be explained by long-standing, generally accepted scientific "facts." Many people experience telepathy, telekinesis, clairvoyance, spontaneous healing, unexplained miracles, and near-death experiences. Our old, limited belief systems simply cannot explain these experiences. We need to expand our concepts and definitions of who we are and what the truth really is in order to explain these mysterious, miraculous, or magical events.

Our Minds Affect the Physical World

Scientists have proven what mystics and spiritual teachers have told us for centuries: Life consists of energy and consciousness that cannot be destroyed; matter is an illusion; and our minds not only affect the physical world, but actually create it. If you examine your hand under a microscope, you will see individual cells. If you looked even more closely at each cell with a more powerful microscope, you would find there is nothing solid about the cell; it is made up of atoms surrounded by a vast amount of space. Upon closer examination of the atom, you find only more space and even smaller subatomic particles called quarks and bosons.

Quantum physics tells us that we are fields of consciousness, energy, and information. There are waves of probabilities, but nothing solid in this field. We are pure consciousness — pure energy in motion; we are not really physical at all! Another amazing discovery is that when an observer focuses his or her attention on this field of energy, particles of light blink into existence. We literally create the appearance of a particle of light through the process of perceiving it. This strongly suggests that our minds not only affect the physical world, but actually help to form it.

All of this may be difficult for some of us to accept because for centuries we have placed our trust in the mechanistic principles of classic physics and biology to explain our reality. According to this mechanistic view of life, the human body is a mere machine that appeared against amazing probabilities, by pure chance and coincidence. Once the machine becomes old or damaged, it begins to disintegrate, and in time it ceases to exist. There is no room in this worldview for the concept of a soul, a human purpose, or an immortal aspect of life. The human mind is seen as the byproduct of a biological, chemical process rather than the product of a conscious soul.

The way we live our lives has not caught up with the latest scientific discoveries. We continue to perceive the world from an old mechanistic point of view based on theories developed hundreds of years ago. Today, the information revealed through quantum physics is astounding. If we could grasp its implications, the way we perceive reality and the way we live our lives would shift dramatically. When we truly understand that we are creators of the world we live in, we will be able to consciously harness our inner power to create the life of our dreams.

If you were alive when the first ocean explorers returned from their voyage and announced that the earth was round, would you refuse to believe them because you had no scientific proof? Would you be excited about the discovery, seeing it as an opportunity to go out and explore the New World for yourself? The people who chose to go beyond their limited perceptions in those days did so at the risk of losing their lives. You won't risk your life if you go beyond your present beliefs, but you may change your life forever.

Are you willing to consider that the beliefs you have held about reality are merely *beliefs* about reality and not necessarily the truth? Are you ready to explore possibilities that exist beyond your currently held versions of reality? Just for a while, be willing to consider the possibility that you are creating all of your experiences in life. Challenge yourself to consider new possibilities. You can always go back to your familiar way of thinking.

part two

Discovering Your Beliefs

"You cannot learn about yourself by studying what is expected of you by others — but only by asking yourself what you expect of yourself, and discovering for yourself in what direction your abilities lie."

—"SETH," JANE ROBERTS, *The Way Toward Health*

three

the origin of beliefs

Most of our beliefs about life have come from parents, teachers, ministers, doctors, and other authority figures as we were growing up. These people were raised on beliefs they received from their authority figures. As time went on, many of these beliefs were completely distorted and untrue, and yet they are often accepted without question by each succeeding generation.

Imagine you are living in the year 2500. There are no longer any historical records in existence because they were all destroyed in 2100, when a severe cosmic storm erased all the historical data that was transferred to computer discs. Now imagine an archeologist uncovering a site from the year 2000. He discovers a large room with a row of cubicles, each containing a white porcelain bowl attached to the floor. There is evidence that these bowls once contained water.

The archeologist, believing that the inhabitants of those times were less advanced, concludes that these cubicles and bowls were used in religious ceremonies, possibly even sacrifices. The fact that there are so many bowls in one location leads him to believe that this must have been a place of worship. He goes on to discover that every single home of these ancient people had at least one of these sacred porcelain bowls carefully sequestered in a separate room. This leads him to believe that this particular religious practice was predominant in the culture of that time. His conclusion: ceremonial rooms rather than bathrooms.

This imaginary story makes an important point: When it comes to authority figures, we cannot always trust what they tell us. Even our history books cannot be trusted to give us an accurate description of what occurred at a given time. History books are rarely written by someone who experienced the historical events directly. What we learn is someone's interpretation of someone else's perception of what happened. The truth could be completely distorted.

Perhaps it's time to question the beliefs we have accepted, especially any limiting beliefs we have about ourselves. Perhaps it's time that we trust our own direct experience and inner knowingness instead of authority figures.

Even authorities who claim to know what is best for us often disagree with one another. Medical theories about what causes cancer change almost daily. It seems that nothing is safe to eat or do anymore. That is why we must learn to listen to our own inner voice and become our own best authority. If we learn to listen to our inner self, we won't be confused by outside authorities who have a tendency to contradict one another anyway.

Concentric Circles

Many of our earliest beliefs were meant to educate us about life and to protect us from danger so that we could function in society and survive in the world. Rules such as "Don't go out into the street; you could get hit by a car" or "Don't touch the stove; you could get burned" were intended to help us survive.

Unfortunately, we sometimes turn these rules into limiting beliefs about reality.

Look at the diagram below and imagine that you are in the middle of many concentric circles.

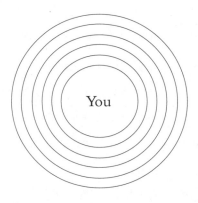

Each circle represents a belief that limits or entraps you. The first circle may have started out as a simple statement: "Don't cross the street by yourself; you could get hit by a car." Most adults outgrow the belief that they can't cross the street by themselves, but they may not realize that the underlying belief has now become: "Life is not safe. I could get hurt."

The second circle may have started out like this: "Don't do that; you're not old enough to do that. You're not old enough to use the stove or to drive a car or to dress yourself." These harmless statements often translate into: "There's something wrong with me. I'm not enough yet." The feeling that we are "not enough yet" often creates workaholics and overachievers who are trying to prove that they are finally enough. It also creates people who are afraid to even try to achieve their dreams because they believe they will never be enough to succeed anyway.

The third circle might have begun like this: "If you tell a lie, or if you break something, or if you don't do your homework, or if you don't eat your vegetables, or if you make me unhappy, you are bad, and I won't love you anymore." Most parents and adults had good intentions when they told us these things. But the belief that often develops as a result of these statements is: "I am bad and, therefore, unlovable."

Parents and society also used rewards and punishments to teach us how to behave. "If you are a good girl, then you can have dessert. As soon as you finish your work, then you can play. If you touch that, you will be sent to your room. If you disappoint me or make me mad, I will withdraw my love from you." Rewards and punishments were originally meant to give us an incentive to learn the rules. Unfortunately, most of us are still using these methods to keep ourselves in line. The old system of reward and punishment continues to limit our lives and our true potential. We won't allow ourselves to have the rewards if we think we are still not enough: not smart enough, not thin enough, not pretty enough, not hardworking enough, not successful enough, not rich enough, not nice enough, and on and on. We continue to punish ourselves if we think we are bad. Often this means withholding something from ourselves that we truly want or need, including love. Our inner dialogue is frequently self-critical, self-degrading, and self-punishing. We believe that by "staying in line," and following the rules and expectations set by others, we will be safe, accepted, and loved. To free ourselves to live our true potential, we must let go of all the fear-based self-judgments that tell us we are bad or not enough.

Many problems in the world are the result of people believing they are basically evil or not good enough. The people who believe they are bad tend to act badly. The people who believe they must steal or take money from others don't believe they are powerful enough, smart enough, or capable enough to make money on their own. The people who try to control, manipulate, or dominate others are the ones who believe they aren't naturally good enough to receive love or respect from others. The people who emphatically and zealously try to get others to agree with the values they uphold are the people who fear they may be wrong. The people who act the most arrogant or self-absorbed are often the most insecure and frightened inside.

The people who believe they are not smart enough or capable enough to know what to do usually give away their power and knowingness. These are the people who expect others to take care of them or to solve all of their problems for them. These people also tend to blame others when things don't work out. People who don't trust and believe in themselves do not live their dreams or achieve their potential.

People who believe they are inherently worthy and can make something of themselves will often reach beyond their circumstances and achieve success despite their physical or mental disabilities. Most successful people have been raised, or raised themselves, to believe that they could accomplish anything.

Protective Walls and Boundaries

Look again at the picture of you in the center of many concentric circles. Each circle represents a limiting belief about yourself or life in general that was meant to protect you. You may now believe that if you stay within the boundaries of these protective walls, you will be safe. If you start to push against or challenge these protective walls, your fears are likely to surface. You may need to transcend your fears and move beyond these walls if you want to change your life or live your dreams.

Imagine yourself as a child sitting on your front lawn. Your mother has told you not to go out into the street because you could get hurt. While you are happily playing in the safety of your yard, all is well. But you soon become tired of the same old surroundings and are no longer content to stay within the yard. As you start to move toward the curb, your mother's voice becomes louder: "Hey, hey, I told you to stay in the yard." As you get closer to the street, your mother's voice gets frantically louder. "I said no! Get away from the street!" The message is translated like this: You'll get hurt if you go outside of your safe boundaries.

As you begin to challenge the limiting beliefs that have kept you safe within a familiar boundary, your inner voice will start to yell at you. Your protective behavior patterns will arise whenever you feel threatened. You may find yourself becoming angry, becoming confused, arguing, yelling, running away, falling asleep, getting sick, becoming frustrated, feeling depressed, shutting down, creating distractions, feeling nervous or anxious, or talking yourself out of moving forward. The phrases: "Yeah but . . ." or "I need to face reality . . ." usually accompany one of your limiting beliefs. "Yeah, but life is hard. Yeah, but I'm not smart enough. I need to face reality; I don't have the money."

If any of your behavior patterns come up while reading this book, then one of your protective walls has been disturbed, threatening one or more of your beliefs. If this occurs, see if you can use this as an opportunity to move through your resistance and identify the belief that is being challenged.

Most people become very upset when their beliefs are threatened. Typically, if something threatens one of our protective walls, we will display our protective behavior pattern, then turn around and stay safely within familiar territory. It is at this point that you can choose to identify the limiting belief and move beyond it, or turn around and keep your life the same as it always has been. Of course, if you always do what you've always done, your life will always be what it is now. Insanity is doing the same thing over and over again, expecting different results each time. If you are happy with your life, keep doing what you've been doing. If you are unhappy, it may be time to go beyond the boundary of what you believe is possible.

You may believe, for example, that if you speak up and express what you feel, others will reject and abandon you. So in order to stay safe within your comfort zone, you suppress your feelings. This is your protective pattern. If you continue to hold this belief, you will continue to suppress yourself. Even if you finally have the courage to speak up, people will abandon you because it is still your belief that they will do so.

First, you need to change your belief that people will abandon you if you express yourself. Start with the simple realization that perhaps not *everyone* will abandon you. Then you must move beyond your familiar protective behavior. You must refuse to withdraw and suppress your feelings. If you stop abandoning you, if you stop discounting yourself, eventually you will experience other people supporting you rather than abandoning you when you speak up. If you don't change your belief and only attempt to change your outer circumstances, you will find yourself struggling against your own invisible walls.

Conditioned Behavior

To demonstrate the principle of conditioned behavior, a large fish tank was divided by a clear sheet of glass, and fish were placed on one side of the tank. As the fish swam around and bumped into the sheet of glass, they learned that this glass was their boundary. Later, the glass was removed, but the fish continued to swim on only one side of the tank. The fish continued to act as if the glass boundary were still there.

A similar experiment was done with fleas placed inside a jar. The fleas tried to jump out of the jar, but they were prevented from escaping by a lid placed on the jar. After a while, the lid was removed, but having learned that they were limited by the lid, the fleas stopped even trying to escape.

This type of conditioned behavior can be found in our own lives as well. We are so conditioned to believe that we are limited, that we often don't bother to discover a reality outside of the one we are accustomed to. All too often we are afraid that if we choose a different path, or if we change our familiar behavior, others will judge us as bad or irresponsible and with-draw their love and approval.

Any rigid definition that we hold about ourself, even if that definition would generally be considered positive, might actually be limiting us. For example, there are people who are proud of their ability to uphold their commitments. On the surface this appears to be a positive thing, but if the commitment is "'til death do us part," they may literally die believing there is no other way out of an unhappy marriage.

Another example: A mother may believe she is a "good parent," but this definition of herself may limit her growth and experiences in life. She may believe that a good parent makes sacrifices for her children and worries about them all the time. She may even take such good care of them that she prevents them from growing and believing in themselves. She may need to expand her definition of what it means to be a good parent, or change the belief that being a "good parent" means she must sacrifice her own needs for her children.

You may believe that you are a very sensitive person — sensitive to certain foods, other people, or environmental elements. You may be proud of this sensitivity and believe it to be a positive quality;

however, this belief may be limiting you in a number of ways. You may fear that you cannot live in certain places, eat the foods you like, or experience certain social activities. If you were to change this belief, you might discover that a whole new world of opportunities is available to you.

four

games and processes

In this chapter you will have the opportunity to discover some of your beliefs by participating in a variety of games and processes. The purpose is to reveal the beliefs that may be limiting you or creating unpleasant experiences.

As you go through these games and processes, notice if any of your behavior patterns begin to emerge. Notice if you feel angry, frustrated, fearful, lost, tired, too busy, distracted, ill, confused, depressed, or argumentative. Once again, if you experience an emotional reaction or one of your protective patterns arises, it may indicate that one or more of your beliefs are being challenged. As you begin to move forward with greater awareness in your life, more of your fears, doubts, and limiting beliefs may come to your attention. A pebble in your shoe is more obvious when you are walking than when you are standing still. Once you discover the pebble, you can clear it out and move with greater ease.

GAME 1
Traveling to Arizona

For this first game, imagine that you have been wanting to travel to the state of Arizona. Of course, if you live in Arizona, please choose a different destination.

Begin this process by imagining that you are sitting in your car somewhere on the side of a road. On the lines below or on a separate piece of paper, describe what you would do to get to Arizona. Your description should be as clear, specific, and honest as possible before going on to the next step.

. . . .

. . . .

. . . .

. . . .

Now take a moment to consider what you have written. Your answers reflect how you are living your life right now; they reveal one or more patterns based on your beliefs. There are no right or wrong answers. Your list simply reveals how you are living your life because of your beliefs.

Next, ask yourself these questions: Are you pleased with where you are in your life right now? Do you usually achieve the most important goals that you set for yourself? If not, you may have restrictive beliefs that cause you to behave in ways that do not support you in reaching your goals.

Here are some examples from participants in my workshops. Notice how their comments reveal their beliefs and patterns of behavior:

1) One woman said she would "just get in her car and drive." In her daily life, this woman has the habit of staying very active and busy. However, she commented that her life is not very fulfilling, and she really isn't sure if her actions are getting her anywhere. Obviously, this approach to life is not working for her. Just getting in her car and driving is not necessarily heading her in the direction of Arizona or her dreams.

This woman discovered that she believes that she must always be active and doing something because otherwise she may appear to be lazy and irresponsible. She feels staying busy is one way for her to validate her existence and her self-worth. Now that she is aware of these beliefs, she can choose to change them.

2) Another woman said she would drive to the nearest town and ask someone for directions. This reveals one of her habitual patterns: her tendency to ask others for their advice. There is nothing wrong with this behavior. But when asked if she was happy with her life and whether she was living her dreams, she said no. Apparently asking others for their opinions and advice was not working for her either. This woman discovered she has a belief that she cannot always trust herself to make the right choices because she has made mistakes in the past. She believes, therefore, that she needs advice from others who may see more clearly than she does or who can validate her feelings and choices.

Let's consider the issue of seeking advice from others. Do you also have the habit of asking others for their advice or opinion? If so, notice what type of person you are asking. Is it a successful person? Is it someone you respect, admire, or trust? If you were asking for directions, would you ask a gas station attendant, a police officer, or the first person you see on the street? Would you prefer to ask an authority? This woman said she would ask the Automobile Association of America for directions. She prefers to ask the advice of legitimate, professional authority figures, people she believes are smarter than she is and trained "to know the right answers."

3) One man answered that before he drove anywhere, he would first check the fuel, the oil, and the water in the car. He would then check to see if he had enough money, food, and supplies to take on his trip. Then he would check a map to see which was the most efficient road to take. This man never got to the point of telling the group he would start driving. What he discovered was that he was spending most of his life *preparing* for his future. He had goals in his life, but didn't feel that he had quite enough money or education to pursue his real dreams. He was still reading books (the map) to prepare himself to do things the "right way."

This man realized that he really hadn't started his journey yet. What beliefs were responsible for stopping him? If he wasn't well prepared, he might not reach his destination. Life will fall apart if he's not careful to build a strong foundation and to consider all the details. He added that his father had led him to believe that he wasn't smart enough to accomplish anything in life. He had figured out that if he just stayed busy preparing for things and never actually moved forward, he would not have to risk failure.

4) A few people answered that they would take their time and choose the most scenic route to Arizona. This is their approach to life. They have decided to simply enjoy the journey and not be in a rush to get anywhere. They believe that life should be enjoyed.

5) Others reported driving to the nearest airport so they could get to Arizona more quickly. This is another obvious reflection of their approach to life. They want to accomplish their goals and reach their destinations as quickly as possible. Their comments: "I don't have time to waste. There is so much to do. Time is money you know. I have to get there quickly." They believe there is never enough time to do everything they need to do, and their experience reflects that belief. They live with constant tension and pressure from all the demands on their time.

6) One person reported fearing that his car might not make it all the way to Arizona. In actuality, this person had been experiencing serious health problems and did not believe that he had the strength to achieve any of his goals. He didn't trust that his body was healthy enough to make the journey.

Notice if your answer revealed anything interesting about your own beliefs and behavior patterns. Did you discover any beliefs such as, "I must be prepared," "I need to have money," "I have to hurry," or "I'd better ask someone else for advice"? Are you just aimlessly "driving" through life, hoping you will someday reach your destination?

Again, if you are happy and fulfilled in your life, if you are easily creating your most cherished desires, your beliefs and habitual actions are working for you. If not, you may want to examine your beliefs to find which ones are not supporting you in attaining your dreams. Your current circumstances can reveal the beliefs that are responsible for creating your experience.

When you began your trip to Arizona, how did you know where you were starting from? Did you look to see the signs that were around you? Even if you looked at a map to see which road to take, you had to know where you were to begin with. If you don't know where your starting point is, it can be difficult to know which way to head.

Take a moment to reflect on your current circumstances, to notice what you have created in your life. What "signs" are telling you where you are now? The first step in accomplishing any goal is to assess your present situation. Then you can move forward with a new vision of the life you have always wanted. The four steps that follow will help you to clarify your present situation and achieve your goals.

1) Observe where you are now. What is and is not working in your life? Consider your personal relationships, career, finances, health, and every other area of your life.

2) Clarify what you want to create in your life. Deep down, we all know what we truly desire to have in life. Many people just lose touch with their true desires because they believe "I can't or I shouldn't have what I want."

3) Believe that you can have what you want. If anyone else has achieved your goal, you can too. If you do

not believe you can or should achieve your dreams, you won't take actions that support you in achieving them.

4) Take action in every possible way: mentally, emotionally, and physically. Mentally visualize achieving your goal. Make the best plan you can think of. Affirm that you are worthy of having everything you desire. Get in touch with what it would feel like to have your dreams come true. For example, how it would feel to have the job you always dreamed of or to be held by someone who loves and adores you? Imagine the gratitude and joy you will feel. Physically take action without doubt or hesitation. Trust your impulses and take whatever action seems right to you. Make that call or write that letter. Do what you can to move forward one step at a time.

If you have a goal that has not yet manifested, review each of these steps to see if one of them is missing from your life.

GAME 2
Color, Animals, Darkness, and Water

In the spaces provided below or on a separate piece of paper, write down three qualities or adjectives that describe the following: (1) Color, (2) Animals, (3) Darkness, and (4) Water.

1) Color (Do not list actual colors such as "blue." Select three words that describe the qualities of color such as "bright.")

. . . .

2) Animals

. . . .

3) Darkness

. . . .

4) Water

. . . .

Now let's look at your answers.

1) The words you chose to describe "color" are words that describe how you perceive yourself. Do you have a better self-image than you thought you had, or is your self-esteem at a low point? Are there any negative self-judgments that could be holding you back?

2) The words you used to describe "animals" reflect your perception of the way others perceive you. Even if others don't perceive you in this way, the words you chose are how *you think* they perceive you. For example, if you described animals as "ferocious and dangerous," you may be afraid that others see you that way. If you believe this, you will interpret their intentions or behavior from that perspective, and your experience will support your beliefs.

3) The words you chose to describe "darkness" are how you perceive death. If you had trouble finding words to describe darkness, you may be uncertain what you believe or how you feel about death. If you chose words such as cold, empty, sad, scary, or other words that evoke loneliness and fear, you may have experienced death as loss.

4) The words you used to describe "water" are how you perceive sex. Do your answers reveal any fear of physical intimacy? Do your answers reflect any problems you have with a current relationship? Are you aware of any issues relating to sex that might stand in the way of a loving, harmonious relationship?

Game 3
People in the Picture

Look at the picture on the next page and choose two people who catch your attention. On the lines below or on a separate piece of paper, write down your thoughts and feelings about each of these people. Who are they? What type of personality does each person have? What is each person feeling, thinking, or considering? Write down anything that you imagine or "sense" about these two people.

. . . .
. . . .
. . . .
. . . .
. . . .

What you wrote about each of these people will reveal something you believe about yourself. Very often we project our thoughts, feelings, beliefs, and self-judgments onto others. What you say about others often says more about you than it does about them.

For example, if you described one person in the picture as happy, carefree, and excited about her future, this is how you perceive yourself right now. If you described

Courtesy of Rail Europe Inc.

another person as impatient, dishonest, or rude, you may fear that you are impatient, dishonest, or rude. If you described someone as warm, loving, and generous, this also describes how you feel about yourself.

If you believe that someone in the picture was exhibiting a certain behavior, but you honestly don't believe you behave that way, ask yourself what that behavior says about the person. What kind of person would act that way? Are you describing qualities that you fear you also possess? In other words, your behavior may not be the same as someone else's, but you may share the same motivation.

For example, if you imagined one of these people to be a thief or a murderer and you know you would not steal from others or want to harm them, explain what kind of person would commit such acts. Is he or she selfish, insecure, evil, weak, stupid, greedy, or fearful? What motivates this type of person? What is your opinion of his or her behavior? Why is it "wrong" or "bad"? If you take an honest look at your opinions about this person, you will discover qualities that you fear you possess or believe you possess also. If you have limiting judgments about yourself, you will limit your power and ability to create what you desire.

GAME 4
The Auto Mechanic

A man dropped off his car at an auto repair garage to have the oil changed. He asked the mechanic to check over the rest of the car while it was there. Shortly after arriving at his office, the man received a call from the mechanic who informed him that his brakes were worn out and in need of replacement. The man thought about it for a moment and then authorized the mechanic to install new brakes. Two hours later, the mechanic called to inform the man that his car needed a new carburetor. The man agreed to pay for a new carburetor. One hour after that call, the man heard from the mechanic again and was told that his car also needed a new ignition switch.

Imagine this scenario for a moment and consider how you would feel if you were in this man's place. On the lines below or on a separate piece of paper, write down what you believe is happening and what the man should do.

. . . .
. . . .
. . . .
. . . .

Remember, there is no right or wrong answer. What you believe is happening to this man and his car, however, reveals some of your own beliefs and behavior patterns.

If you told the man to get a second opinion, you probably ask others for their opinions or advice. Not trusting the mechanic shows that you have a basic mistrust of others. What it ultimately reveals, however, is that you don't trust yourself.

One woman said that she would go down to the garage and see for herself what the damaged parts looked like before she would allow the mechanic to continue. This is how this woman conducts her life. She wants to be in control of her life at all times. She is a perfectionist, preferring to do everything herself. She doesn't trust that others can do things as well as she can. Although there is nothing wrong with her choices, she typically spends her time working very hard, trying to make everything perfect. When someone needs to be in control all the time, it reflects a basic mistrust of self, of others, and of life in general. This woman had a fear that she was somehow "bad" and that things could go out of control if she didn't stay on top of her life at all times.

Another woman answered that she would trust the mechanic's advice and allow him to fix whatever he found wrong with the car. This woman lives her life trusting others. She believes that everything always works out for her highest good, so she doesn't worry about anything or struggle against seeming injustices. She trusts life. "Things happen for a good reason," she told us, and for some odd reason, things always work out for her. At least that is *her* perception. She certainly seems to enjoy life more than most people, so this belief works for her.

What are your thoughts about this latter woman's response? Are you inspired by her story or do you feel critical and mistrustful of the way she handles her life? Do you find yourself saying, "Yeah, but she may run out of money some day and regret her carefree, frivolous attitude" or "Yeah, but she may not be facing reality by being so trusting and naive"? If so, your judgments of her behavior reflect your self-judgments as well.

One young man commented that it seemed the mechanic wanted his car, so he said that he would probably just give the car to the mechanic. This seemed to be a very unusual answer, until we learned from this young man that he had an incurable disease and was not expected to live much longer. He felt that God wanted him to come home, and he had decided not to fight his illness any longer.

Months after completing this exercise, one woman commented that before the workshop she had a history of dealing with dishonest auto mechanics. After she realized that her beliefs would continue to be reflected in her experience, she focused on changing her beliefs. Since then, she has had nothing but positive experiences with her auto mechanic.

GAME 5
The Soul Partner

A woman we will call Katrina met with a friend for lunch one day. Katrina told her friend that she was frustrated and confused about her current situation. She had been longing for a loving relationship in her life and had recently met an extraordinary man. Katrina loved being with this man. They had a fabulous time whenever they were together. She found him easy to talk to, and they loved to do the same things. He was good-looking, intelligent, caring, and considerate — everything she had ever wanted in a man. She even felt he might be her soul mate. However, this man constantly traveled out of town. Photography was his main interest, and he loved to visit places where he could take fascinating and unusual pictures.

Katrina explained that her job kept her from traveling with him, but she noted that he had never really asked her to accompany him on any of his trips. She loved spending time with this man, but she was unhappy about the small amount of time they actually had together.

Before meeting this man, Katrina had been dating another man who was very much in love with her and wanted to marry her. She explained that this man was a wonderful, sensitive, and wealthy businessman, but they did not have much in common. Although they had enjoyable times together, she didn't feel they had much to talk about. Katrina expressed her concern about her situation and told her friend that she wasn't sure what to do.

If you were Katrina's friend and she asked you for advice, what would you tell her? Would your answer be different if you knew she had been seeing the first man she had dated (the businessman) for two years? What if they had dated for five or six years? Please take

a moment to consider what you would say to Katrina.
Then write down your comments.

. . . .
. . . .
. . . .
. . . .

The advice you gave to Katrina reflects the same
advice that you are giving to yourself about something
that is currently happening in your life. Your answer
may reveal that you feel you need to choose between
your life dream (the soul mate) or settling for less
than your dreams because it is safer, easier, or more
convenient.

Did your answer change when you thought Katrina had known the businessman for a much longer
time? Since she had already invested many years in
this relationship, were you more willing to encourage
her to work things out, or were you afraid that too
much time had already been wasted? Why or why
not? Did your answer reflect any feelings of guilt or
obligation toward the businessman? If so, are the
choices you are currently making founded on guilt or
a sense of obligation?

One man in class answered that he thought Katrina should stay with the businessman because in time she may learn to love him even though the other man seemed to be her soul mate. He said he thought that working things out with the photographer might take too much effort and might not be worth the risk. This man finally revealed his deep desire to work in a field which could help save and protect the environment. He was afraid, however, to leave his secure job with an accounting firm, and kept hoping that in time he would learn to love the job. This man believed that his desire to work with the environment was "probably just a dream and would never become a reality."

Another man answered that Katrina should be honest and speak openly with the photographer. He believed that sincere and loving communication was the key. With enough patience and commitment, he felt they would be able to work things out. His reply gave him the solution he was looking for to deal with his own marriage difficulties.

One of the women in class answered that she thought Katrina should keep looking because neither man was right for her. This woman admitted that she didn't believe she had found her life's work or her life's purpose yet. She was preparing to quit her job so that she could continue looking for a career that would make her happy.

Now remember, the advice you gave Katrina will reflect your own beliefs. This doesn't mean that your advice is the only available solution to your own situation or dilemma. A multitude of solutions are available to you unless you believe you have limited options.

We can use stories such as this one to help us discover our own issues and solutions. If we listen carefully to the advice we give to others, we will hear our own best advice based on our beliefs. It is often much easier to give advice to others because we can view their circumstances more objectively. When the challenge we are facing is our own, we may not always think clearly or come up with the best solutions. We may be traumatized by the situation or have an emotional attachment to a particular outcome. When we are emotionally attached to a particular outcome, we cannot see the situation clearly. Our emotions can cloud our thinking and our intuition.

If you observe your reactions to other people's situations, or even observe your reactions to movies or television dramas, you can gain insights into your own beliefs and self-judgments. All judgments about others reflect our own self-judgments. If you have an issue with someone, that person is showing you something about yourself that you do not like. The next time someone exhibits a personality trait or emotional quality that upsets you, ask yourself if you have a similar judgment about yourself. This also means that if you admire someone for a particular quality such as warmth or generosity, deep down you feel you also possess this quality.

Your feelings and self-judgments can serve as tools to help you discover your beliefs. Making a judgment, however, is different from making an observation. Making a judgment indicates that you have an issue with yourself; an observation does not. To know whether you are making a judgment about someone or merely an observation, use these standards to distinguish between the two: If a person's behavior evokes an emotional response from you, whether positive or negative, you are making a judgment. If you believe a situation or particular behavior is good or bad, right or wrong, you are making a judgment. Don't feel that you should suppress your feelings or pretend that you don't have any judgments. Allow yourself to feel whatever you feel so that you can discover your beliefs and self-judgments. When you don't have an emotional response or judgment about someone's behavior, your response is likely to be "That's interesting." This type of response indicates you are only making an observation.

GAME 6
The Backpack

A man wanted to buy his daughter a backpack for her birthday. He wasn't sure if he should buy a yellow backpack or a pink one. He finally decided to buy her a pink backpack.

What is your response to this story? Please take a moment to write down your thoughts and feelings.

. . . .
. . . .
. . . .
. . . .

If your response was anything other than "That's interesting" or "So what?" then your reaction to his choice — that is, your judgment of his behavior — reflects something in your own life that you have a similar judgment about.

One woman became upset with this simple story and commented that the man should have given his daughter a choice. Upon deeper examination, we discovered that the woman felt that she was domineering and always needed to have everything her way. Recently, she had not allowed her nineteen-year-old son to go away with his friends for the weekend. She was afraid that she had been too controlling by not allowing him to make his own choices.

Another woman was incensed that this man would make such an obviously chauvinistic statement by buying a pink backpack just because the child was a girl. We discovered that this woman had been carrying some of her own chauvinistic ideas about life. She was angry with her husband for not being the responsible and traditional breadwinner, and she was angry with herself for feeling the way she did. In her eyes, she was holding on to an outdated idea and she was embarrassed that she wasn't as open-minded or as modern as she wanted to be.

For those of you who were not bothered by this man's decision, your answer would have simply been "That's interesting" or "So what?" As you begin to clear up some of your own self-judgments, your response to many of life's situations will be "That's interesting."

With your mind free from the clutter of self-judgments, you will find more to be grateful for in life. You will experience more joy, more lightness, more freedom. Self-judgments and constant upsets make life seem heavy and difficult. The less time you spend criticizing yourself and others, the more time you will have to enjoy life. The fewer self-judgments you have, the more you can use your creative power, realize your divinity, and make your dreams come true.

GAME 7
Perception and Beliefs

Our beliefs affect our perceptions, which in turn create our experiences. Our beliefs act like filters that allow only certain kinds of information to permeate our mind. We perceive life through these filters; we see life through the "colored lenses" of our beliefs.

Look around you right now and notice everything you see that is blue. Close your eyes and make a mental list of everything that was blue, then open your eyes and look around to see if you missed anything.

Now close your eyes again. Without peaking, remember everything you saw that was yellow. Open your eyes and look around. Did you miss anything? Chances are you didn't notice any yellow objects in your environment because you were looking for blue objects. The yellow objects were in plain sight while you were looking for the blue objects, but you probably didn't notice them because your attention was focused on the blue objects. Whatever you are looking for is what you are likely to find. If you believe that something is true, you will perceive life from that perspective.

If you believe, for example, that your childhood was unhappy, you will only find evidence to support that belief when you look at your past. Even if there were many times as a child that you were happy, your belief in an unhappy childhood won't allow you to remember the happy times at all. If you have a belief that you are loved, safe, and provided for, you will perceive all your experiences in that light. If your beliefs are based on fear, suspicion, and doubt, no matter what good fortune may occur in your life, you will be full of mistrust and fear.

Now think of a watch that you own. Without looking at your watch, remember everything you can about its appearance. Is it digital, or does it have hands? What do the hands look like? Does it have a second hand? What color are the hands? Are there Arabic numbers on the face, Roman numerals, or just plain lines to note the hour? Are the numbers or lines at 3, 6, 9, and 12, or are all the numbers on the face? Is there any writing on the face of your watch? What does it say? Is the manufacturer's name on the watch? What is it? What color is the face? Is there a date?

Take a close look at your watch. Did you miss anything? Now look away from your watch again. What time is it? Although you just looked at your timepiece, chances are you cannot answer this question. You probably look at your watch many times throughout the day, and yet you may not have remembered what it looks like. That's because when you look at your watch, you typically want to know what time it is, and that is what you notice. When you looked at your watch just now, however, your intention was to notice its appearance, not the time.

Again, your perception is limited to what you are looking for. Whatever you believe is what you will see and experience.

GAME 8
The Reckless Driver

Imagine that you are driving along a highway when someone suddenly cuts in front of you. How would you react? The way you interpret the driver's actions — the way you perceive and experience the incident — will depend upon your beliefs. Let's consider a variety of responses to this one incident.

One possible reaction is this: "What an irresponsible, reckless jerk! He could hurt someone. He obviously doesn't care about anyone but himself."

A second possible reaction could be: "Wow! That driver is sure in a hurry. He should slow down and enjoy life."

A third reaction might be: "Everything always happens for my benefit, so I guess that driver cut in front of me for a reason. Maybe I need to slow down because there is a highway patrol car ahead. Maybe I have avoided an accident because I was forced to slow down."

A fourth perspective could be: "That person seems very upset and oblivious to his surroundings. I wonder if something terrible just happened in his life. I hope he will be okay."

Now consider what your own reaction would have been. You probably will never know what was going on with the other driver, but you can learn from the experience by noticing your response to the event. The way you experience anything that happens in your life has little to do with anyone else's reality. It has everything to do with your own beliefs and perceptions. It doesn't matter what a person's actions are, you will interpret and experience his or her actions through the "colored lenses" of your own beliefs.

Every challenge in your life is an opportunity to discover your beliefs and to choose those that work for you instead of against you. You will naturally attract people and situations into your life that reflect your own issues and self-judgments.

GAME 9
What's Bothering Me?

Here is a simple technique you can use to help you to become aware of your self-judgments and to resolve an unpleasant issue with someone else. These four simple questions can shed light on your beliefs and offer an entirely new perspective on the problem.

When you answer the four questions, don't rely on the examples given or try to guess what you *should* say. If you want to know what is really going on inside your mind, your answers must be honest.

Think of someone whose behavior is bothering you. It may be a spouse, a parent, a child, a relative, a boss, or a friend. Take four pieces of paper and write one of these four questions at the top of each page.

1) What bothers me about this person? What is he or she doing that upsets me?

2) Why is he or she behaving this way? What do I believe is the real, underlying reason for his or her behavior?

3) What would I like to say to this person? If I could say anything at all that might help change this person's behavior, what would it be?

4) What do I want from this person?

Please take a few moments to write your answers to each of these questions. Take your time, and be as thorough and honest as possible. Write down every answer you can think of. State clear and simple answers; don't spend time recounting a specific incident or telling stories. Stating precise answers will make you become aware of the true problem as well as the best solution to the problem. Here is an example of one woman's response to the questions:

1) What bothers me about John? What is he doing that upsets me?

He is not listening to me. He doesn't respect me. He nags me and bosses me around. He always criticizes me. He is not considerate of my feelings. He doesn't spend enough time with me. He's mean. He's arrogant and selfish. He's a procrastinator. He doesn't do what he says he will do.

2) Why is he behaving this way? What do I believe is the real, underlying reason for his behavior?

He's probably afraid no one likes him. He's trying to protect himself. He's afraid of being rejected, so he's pushing people away. He's very insecure. He doesn't believe in himself. He's afraid of failure, afraid of losing his job. He's really tired and feels unappreciated. He had a difficult childhood, and he is continuing to make things difficult for himself.

3) What would I like to say to him? If I could say anything at all that might help change his behavior, what would it be?

Please listen to me. I wish you would stop hurting my feelings. Don't worry about money or about losing your job; everything will be fine. Please spend more time with me. Keep your word, and do what you say you're going to do.

4) What do I want from him?

I want him to respect me, to believe in me, to spend more time with me, and to love me. I also want him to tell me nice things, to get off my back and stop criticizing me, and to have more fun with me.

Now that you have written your honest answers, look them over and consider them from this perspective: Who you are talking to is yourself.

1) What bothers me about this person? What is he or she doing that upsets me?

These are the things that you don't like about yourself. These are the judgments you have about yourself.

2) Why is he or she behaving this way? What do I believe is the real, underlying reason for his or her behavior?

This is your deeper, underlying reason for behaving this way.

3) What would I like to say to him or her? If I could say anything at all that might help change this person's behavior, what would it be?

This is what your inner self is saying to you. If you listen, your life will change dramatically.

4) What do I want from this person?

This is what you need to give to yourself or do for yourself to make your life more fulfilling. If you do these things for yourself, other people in your life will also begin to treat you differently. If you want someone to stop abandoning you, you need to stop abandoning yourself. If you want someone to love you unconditionally, you need to love yourself unconditionally. If you want someone to listen to you, you need to listen to yourself. If you want someone to honor your feelings, you need to honor yourself. If you want someone to keep his or her word, you need to keep your word to yourself. If you want someone to spend more time with you, you need to spend more time with yourself. You may feel that you do spend lots of time with yourself, but is it quality time or quiet time that you spend with yourself, or are you always busy when you spend time alone?

If someone criticizes you and it upsets you, this is because you are criticizing yourself. If people are giving you conflicting advice and mixed messages, this is because you are giving yourself conflicting advice and mixed messages. If it bothers you when you feel that others don't believe in you or support you, this is because you don't believe in yourself or support yourself.

The relationships in your life are your greatest mirrors. Others will always treat you the way you are treating yourself. They will say aloud to you the things you say silently to yourself. They will act out your inner beliefs and fears. If you do not like how people are treating you, change how you are treating yourself. If you don't have an issue with yourself, people will treat you well, or their words and actions will not affect you.

Again, if someone does something that causes you to react, this is really an issue you have with yourself. You will know it's his or her issue and not your own if you do not have an emotional reaction or a judgment. Imagine someone approaching you and telling you that your hair is purple. Because you know your hair is not purple, your response might be, "That's interesting. I wonder what is going on with him today?" It's unlikely that his comment would cause you much pain or upset you if you didn't believe there was something wrong with your hair. But suppose someone says, "You look like you've gained some weight," and you have a judgment about the extra pounds you have put on. This comment is likely to elicit an emotional response such as guilt, shame, anger, embarrassment, or frustration. Your emotional reaction is a clue to one of your own self-judgments or an underlying belief that is causing you pain.

part three

Changing Your Beliefs

"Argue for your limitations, and sure enough, they're yours."

—RICHARD BACH, *Illusions*

five

methods for changing
your beliefs

When something in our life makes us unhappy, we often attempt to change the outer circumstances: quit the job, get a divorce, move to another city, go on a diet. We have been taught to fix things outside of us, when we really need to change our inner beliefs. If we don't change our beliefs, we create the same circumstances again and again. When the same situations keep occurring, this only reinforces our belief that this is the only reality there is. It's an endless cycle until we stop the process by questioning and changing our beliefs.

To change your experience, you need to change your beliefs. It does no good to try to change other people or outer circumstances because your beliefs will continue to create the same circumstances in your life. You can leave an unhappy relationship or quit an unpleasant job, but if you maintain the same beliefs, you will continue to attract similar situations and people no matter where you go. You simply can't run away from you. Your life is a mirror of your beliefs.

For example, if you have a habit of choosing partners who are emotionally wounded, you will most likely continue this pattern until you change your need to rescue others. If you are not feeling appreciated at your place of employment, chances are you will experience similar circumstances at other jobs as well. This is not to say you should never change jobs or get a divorce; your job or your marriage may no longer support who you are. But you must realize that changing jobs or partners does not guarantee that you will solve your problems.

You can walk away from your current "mirror," but you will still see your own reflection when you stand in front of the next one. You must change who you are in order to see a new reflection in the mirror.

Only when you change some of your beliefs before you enter into a new relationship or a new job, will you create a new experience.

Believe that You Can Do It

Most people would find it easy to write a letter but difficult or impossible to build a house or create a large sum of money. Others find that making money is no problem for them, but finding a partner is a constant dilemma. There are people who have no problem finding a partner; their greatest challenge is making enough money to pay their bills. The degree of difficulty in creating what we want lies within our belief about the difficulty or possibility of creating it.

When it comes to creating a new experience, we need to believe it is possible to create something other than what presently exists in our lives. Too often we believe that whatever exists right now is hard, factual reality and that anything else we may hope for is wishful thinking or fantasy.

Most people have no problem believing they can drive a car. But imagine what would happen if someone believed that it was difficult or even impossible to learn how to drive. When you expect that you can learn to drive, you take action to create that experience. If you believe you cannot drive, why would you even try? If you have a belief that only one course of action is possible, it won't even occur to you to look for a different course of action. Your limited belief will limit your experience.

Changing a belief doesn't have to be difficult or take a long time. When you find a belief that is limiting you, simply choose another belief. Imagine that you can turn the dial on your "mental radio" and tune into a new frequency. Focus on more desirable, more empowering, and more inspiring thoughts. You may think this is difficult to do, but it will only be so if you believe that it is.

Here's a simple experiment you can do: Think about a yellow pencil. Now, stop thinking about the yellow pencil and think instead about a red rose. Was it difficult to stop thinking about the yellow pencil and start thinking about the red rose? That's how simple it can be to change your thoughts and beliefs.

It was once believed that eggs were good for you to eat. Later, authorities declared that eggs cause high cholesterol and are not healthy for you. Instantly, millions of people changed their belief and stopped or reduced their consumption of eggs. As you can see, it is possible for people to change beliefs, literally overnight.

Now, if you have spent a lifetime focusing on yellow pencils or believing in a particular problem, it could be a little more challenging to break this habit. It may be difficult, for example, to affirm that you are prosperous when you are sitting before a pile of unpaid bills. Because you have reinforced your old belief for so long, you will likely have a great deal of evidence to support it. Until you have reinforced the new, desirable belief by finding evidence to support it, you will be tempted to return to your old patterns.

Every belief also generates its own emotional state. We can become addicted to the familiar feelings that accompany our beliefs, making it more challenging to change that belief. It can be easier to stay in a comfortable rut than to move on and forge a new path. At least we know what to expect with the old familiar beliefs and emotions, even if they are unpleasant. Sometimes we love the passion, the intensity, and the drama of emotions. Once we start feeling sorry for ourself, feeling depressed, or feeling angry, these emotions gain momentum and can take on a life of their own. We can think of emotions as "energy in motion." Once an emotion is actively engaged, it can be challenging to stop it.

Changing your beliefs will take focus, determination, commitment, concentration, and discipline. You must keep your attention focused on your new, desired situation and not allow yourself to lazily slip back into old, comfortable ways. It may take effort in the beginning, but with practice it does get easier. Everything we learn takes practice: walking, talking, eating, writing, riding a bicycle, driving, and so on. So practice, practice, practice. Soon your new belief will feel as comfortable and familiar as the old one.

While you are changing your beliefs, your life may appear to be in chaos for a while, as two opposing beliefs vie for position in your world. You may experience static on your new "mental station" until you are able to successfully adjust the dial and stabilize the frequency. Your old life experience may continue for a while, but this doesn't mean that the process isn't working. Don't give up. Even though it may be challenging at times, it is still a worthwhile endeavor.

Find Evidence to Support Your New Belief

When you have a belief, you will find evidence to support that belief. One of the ways to change a belief is to choose a new belief, find evidence to support the new belief, then begin to act as if this belief is true for you.

Here are some examples: If you have a judgment that you are stupid and make mistakes, look for evidence to support the belief that you are smart and have made good choices. Look for evidence to support the idea that the choices you made eventually worked out for the best or that you learned something from making those choices. Write down a list of the new evidence so you can look at it whenever you need to remind yourself that you are smart. The more attention you give to the new belief, the easier it will be to release the old belief.

Next begin to act with a newfound confidence, believing that you do know how to make wise choices. Don't be afraid to make decisions or choices; support yourself no matter what choice you make. The choices you make will rarely be life-threatening, so it may help to relax and take life less seriously.

If you have a fear of being in a relationship because you believe that relationships end in painful separations, find examples of couples who have lived together in love and harmony for years. Look for evidence to support the belief that not all relationships are unhappy. Many couples have lived together their entire lives and still love and honor each other. Find evidence that not all relationships end in pain. Look for people who have gone through separations easily and amicably. Some people have not only survived separations, but are actually happier since their separations. If you have a fear of experiencing pain, you will create what you fear. Next, begin to act as if you are in a happy, fulfilling relationship.

If you believe that finding a job is difficult and you doubt that anyone would hire you, remember a time when someone did hire you. Feel the same confidence and remember what you did when you were hired for that job. Gather evidence to support the idea that you are even more valuable now because you have more knowledge and experience than you did before. If you believe that your age is a detriment, remember that many of the world's most accomplished men and women were in their later years when they completed their greatest work.

If you were an employer, would you hire someone like you? If you would, then imagine someone

else feeling the same way about you for the same reasons. If you wouldn't hire someone like you, why not?
What don't you like about yourself? You have the
ability and the power to change. You are in charge of
creating yourself. Make sure that you focus predomi-
nantly on your positive qualities and the fact that you
are a desirable employee.

If you believe that you cannot create abundance in
your life, look for evidence of those times when you
have had money or other forms of abundance. You
need to start somewhere, no matter how small or
feeble your evidence may be. Look for evidence to
prove the opposite belief, the belief that you have
been able to create some wonderful things in your
life so that you can begin to build a new confidence
and with it a new experience. Then begin to act
as if you have abundance. This may be as simple as
spending a little more money when you would usually
spend less.

You may fear that by pretending you are happy or
abundant you will not receive more love, more
money, or more of anything you want. Many people
were raised to believe that if they have plenty, they
don't deserve or shouldn't ask for more. For example,

"You already have a lot of toys, you shouldn't ask for more on your birthday."

The law of manifestation works this way: Like attracts like. If you radiate wealth and abundance, you will attract wealth and abundance. If you radiate love, you will attract more love. If you feel successful, happy, lovable, healthy, and wealthy, you attract these things to you. Whatever you send out will come back to you in like kind.

Use Your Imagination

Your imagination is a powerful tool for creating the mental pictures that will strengthen your new beliefs. By imagining your new pictures, you send directions to your inner self, which knows how to create and bring these pictures into physical form.

Often we fear that the new belief is just wishful thinking or that we are fooling ourselves, so we stop imagining the new. The fear of being hurt or disappointed can also keep us from believing that a better situation will arise. To adamantly insist that the old situation is the only reality available to you, however, will not change your circumstances. By continuing to affirm that you are poor, for example, you will continue to experience lack. You will not even allow your inner self to come up with new ideas to change your circumstances for the better.

You must take steps to reinforce the new belief so a new experience can emerge. As you focus on the belief that you are prosperous, begin to imagine the feelings that go along with your new prosperity. Imagine how good it feels to pay the stack of bills sitting before you. This does not mean that you deny the bills exist; it means that you now believe you are prosperous, and that the bills will soon be completely paid off. Your mind will then automatically look for ways that this can happen. As each bill is paid, see this as further confirmation that your new belief is true. Even if you only find a dime on the street, imagine it is proof that money is coming to you.

It's important when you fantasize about your new situation that you don't work against yourself by doubting that your dreams can come true. When you visualize and imagine, you must truly feel that your desires will manifest. Focus on feeling and sensing the full experience of what it is like to live your dreams.

If money has been a problem for you, imagine having abundance in your life. Feel this new experience physically, emotionally, and mentally. Spend time imagining your new, abundant life until you can believe this idea is not only possible, but highly probable. Don't restrict your imagination by trying to be realistic; the inner self will discover new possibilities for you to create abundance. Also, notice what feelings arise while you are imagining your new abundance. Do you feel guilty, bad, unworthy, or selfish? These feelings will give you clues to beliefs that might sabotage your ability to create wealth and abundance.

If you have had difficulty finding or maintaining a loving relationship, imagine yourself being loved, comforted, and nurtured by a wonderful partner. Give your inner self a clear picture of what you want so it knows what to create for you. Imagine speaking with this person. How does it feel to have a loving partner talk to you with sincerity and appreciation? How does it feel to have this person's arms around you? Do you feel ecstatic, grateful, warm?

Also notice if you are afraid to let yourself imagine this relationship. Are you afraid to "get your hopes up" because you fear that you may be disappointed? Do you believe that things don't always work out for you? Are you assuming that whatever happened in your past is destined to happen again in your future? Are you afraid of being rejected or abandoned if you allow yourself to be open and trusting? Notice what fearful beliefs you may have, because they will create what you fear.

You can also use your imagination to move through any fears that you may have. Imagine splitting up from a loved one or losing your job. What would you experience and how would you feel? What would happen after that? Then what would happen? Keep looking past each experience until you move through the fear.

Do you have a fear of running out of money? Imagine having no money right now. What do you see? Are you living on the streets? Are you living at a homeless shelter? Did you move in with your parents or children? What might really happen? Then what happens? What happens after that? Use your imagination to envision the future, and eventually you will find humor in the absurdity of the situation or you will feel calmer and more at ease with the outcome. When you face the fear, you can move through it and past it. This exercise will dissipate the energy around the fear. You will probably discover that you are a better survivor, and a more creative problem solver, than you thought.

Watch What You Say

Another way to change old, limiting beliefs is to stop reinforcing them by talking about them. Carefully select what you talk about and the words you use. When you don't talk about your problems, you change the focus of your thoughts, which will ultimately affect your experience.

If you constantly complain about how terrible life is, you will continue to experience a terrible life. If you complain, criticize, and gossip, your mental energy and inner pictures will be focused upon those things and will only create more of the same situations. Talk about and reinforce the new, unlimited concepts that you want to create in your life. If you talk about how wonderful your life is and how grateful you are for everything, your thoughts will follow that flow of consciousness and begin to create those situations.

People are often afraid they won't have anything to say if they don't talk about their problems. They may also fear that others won't feel sorry for them and therefore won't care about them anymore. If you didn't talk about your problems, what would you talk about? If you aren't focusing on your problems, you will have more energy and time to focus on creating what you do want.

Also notice your choice of words. Your inner self takes your words quite literally. If you use phrases such as: "I am tired of," "I'm sick of," or "I'm dying to," your inner self will follow your directions and create a situation in which you are tired, sick, or dying.

Certain words, when used habitually, reinforce the faulty belief that life is a constant struggle and our choices are limited. Here is a sample of some of them:

Victim and struggle words	Empowering words
I *should* do this	I *choose* to do this
I *have* to do this	I *have the desire* to do this
I *ought* to do this	I *will* do this
I will *try* to do this	I *am* focusing on doing this
It's *hard* work and a struggle	It's *easy* and effortless

To demonstrate the difference between certain words, close your eyes and imagine yourself at work *trying* to get something done by 5:00 P.M. Notice how you feel and what you are thinking and doing. Now see yourself at work *focusing* on getting something done by 5:00 P.M. Do you notice any difference in the way each word makes you feel? "Trying" is more likely to be associated with stress, panic, and frenzied energy. "Focusing" implies a calmer, sharper, more lucid approach to the task, making it easier to accomplish.

If you tell yourself, "I'll try," your mind doesn't know what to do with this word. You didn't tell yourself to *do* it; you told yourself to just *try*. If you tell yourself, "I will," your mind knows how to act on your will. When you say, "I'll try," you are expressing inner conflict, struggle, and a fear of failure or doubt that you can do something.

If you say you "should" do something, you may be setting yourself up for self-judgment. You may consider yourself irresponsible or bad if you don't do it. If you say you "have to" do something, you are implying you have no choice. If you say "I *choose* to do it," you are saying that you are the one in charge, the one who makes the choices, the master of your own life.

Clear Out Conflicting Beliefs

While we may want to have a certain experience, we may also believe that it isn't possible. Conflicting beliefs create confusion and frustration. When we give mixed messages to our inner power, we get mixed results. We may eventually attain our dreams, but not without struggle and conflict.

To create our desires with ease and joy, we must become aware of any beliefs that tell us that we can't or shouldn't have what we want. We must consciously choose the beliefs that support our desires and strengthen our purpose. If you have a desire to win the lottery but have a deep belief that it probably won't happen, then you probably will not win the lottery.

If you believe that obtaining money without hard work is wrong, then even if you do win the lottery, you are likely to feel guilty, sabotage your success, and lose the money somehow. If you want to create a fulfilling career, a loving relationship, or an abundance of money, you must believe that what you want is possible and trust that you can have it.

There is another reason why you may not have what you want in your life. You may be unhappy with some conditions in your life right now, but you may be choosing them unconsciously because of the benefits you gain from those circumstances.

For example, if you are in poor health, you may unconsciously believe that there are more benefits to being ill than well. You may believe you will receive more love and attention if you are ill, or that others will not ask or expect as much from you. Perhaps being ill is the only acceptable excuse you allow yourself when you want to slow down and stop working so hard.

If you are afraid to take certain risks in life, being ill may give you a valid excuse not to take those risks. Maybe you believe that you are unworthy and don't deserve to be happy, and this is how you punish yourself. So all the time you may think you want to be healthy, when in truth, you have a conflicting belief that you are better off being sick. In order to have what you desire, you need to believe there is more benefit in having it than in not having it.

Many people want a loving relationship, but they have a conflicting belief that they are unworthy or unlovable. They may believe that life never works out for them, or that relationships are hard to find. With these opposing ideas, they continue to struggle with relationships. If you are single and have struggled for years to find the "right one," you may believe there are more benefits to being single than to being in a committed relationship. Perhaps freedom is important to you, and you believe that being single offers you more freedom. Maybe you feel it is safer to be single than to face the potential heartache of rejection or abandonment. You may feel that you will experience less conflict or pain if there is no one around all the time who can point out your flaws. Perhaps you believe that all relationships are like your parents' relationship, and you don't want to experience that type of relationship.

Often, if you have a fear of commitment or a fear of being trapped in a relationship, you will attract someone who has the same issue. You will create a relationship that is "safe." You may find yourself attracted to someone who lives far away, who is already involved in another relationship, who travels a lot, or who also has a fear of commitment. In this way, you can avoid being trapped or making a long-term commitment yourself. If you think your attraction to this person is accidental, it is not. Even if you are not consciously aware of a person's circumstances, you will attract your perfect mirror — someone who reflects your beliefs. If you want someone who is willing to make a commitment, you must be willing to make a commitment.

One way to clear out conflicting beliefs is to do the following exercise. Take out three pieces of paper so you can write down your answers. Think of something that you would like to have in your life. For example: more money, a loving relationship, a vacation, a healthier body, more time for yourself. At the top of the first page, write down whatever it is that you dream of having.

On this first page, also write the words, "I don't really want it because . . ." Under this heading, make a list of all the unpleasant things that may go along with having what you want. For example, if you want more money, the unpleasant things that might come with having more money may be worrying about investments, more taxes, more responsibility, jealous friends, or needy relatives who may expect a handout from you. Whatever pops into your head, write it down. Don't analyze or talk yourself out of any idea that arises. If it comes up, it's on your mind. Write it down so you can deal with it. Be thorough; you want to be sure to reveal any beliefs that might prevent you from achieving your desire. Do this part of the exercise now.

When you have listed everything you can think of, write five more answers on this list. Do this now.

Now, write five more answers. What thoughts and feelings come up for you as you're told to write more? Do you become frustrated, impatient, or rebellious? Do you feel stuck? Do you feel confused or hopeless? Notice what self-defeating behavior patterns arise so that you can move past them.

At the top of page two, write the words, "I can't have it. I'm not enough."

Under this heading, list all the reasons you believe you are not able to have what you want right now, today, this moment. For example, if you want more money, you may not believe it's possible to have it right now because you haven't worked hard enough or long enough, or you're not as lucky as some people who have inherited it, or you've been too lazy to work hard, or you weren't wise enough to start investing a long time ago, or you don't know how to make a lot of money. Do you believe that you can't have what you want right now, this instant, because "that's not how life works," because it's not "realistic"? How does life work according to your beliefs? Is it hard work? Will it take a long time?

Remember, these are just beliefs you have about the nature of reality. Even if there is plenty of evidence in your life to support those beliefs, they are not necessarily the truth. Write down every reason you can think of.

At the top of page three, write the words, "I shouldn't have it. I'm bad." Under this heading, list what you fear you might become if you had what you want, then list any reasons why you shouldn't have it yet. If you have difficulty thinking of any reasons why you shouldn't have what you want, write down any-thing and everything that you don't like about others who have it and you will have the judgments that belong on this list. Are you afraid you might become selfish, lazy, or bored? Do you feel you haven't paid your dues or haven't worked hard enough yet? Would others feel jealous or inferior, and you don't want to hurt their pride or their feelings? What would that say about you? What kind of terrible person do you think you are that you are capable of hurting others? Are you afraid that you are secretly mean and self-centered, concerned only with your own happiness? Do you think you would lose your motivation and not want to accomplish anything? Are you afraid you would become an arrogant know-it-all? Do you believe that attaining your desire will mean you are less spiritual? Again, be thorough with your answers.

Now, let's begin to clear some of these limiting beliefs. Remember, if you believe you are bad or "not enough," you will limit your divine power to make your dreams come true. Listed below are some of the steps you can take to take to change your beliefs, perceptions, and attitudes.

Step 1

First, scan your list of reasons under "I don't really want it." If you have a long list, it's no wonder you haven't created this desire in your life! Look at all the beliefs that are contrary to your desire. Then look at each of your answers and ask yourself: "Are you sure you don't really want that?" For example, if you believe that friends or relatives will begin to ask you for money, are you certain that you won't like giving them money? This first step will reveal some of the reasons why you don't have what you want right now.

Step 2

Imagine a different scenario. Change your expectations of what could possibly happen if you have what you want right now. For example, if you don't like the idea of having a lot of money because you believe it will require too much effort to deal with it, use your imagination to change the picture. Imagine finding a wonderful, trustworthy accountant or financial advisor who loves what she does and is an expert at helping you invest your money. Now, if you don't trust accountants, you have another belief to examine. Remember, if you don't trust others, this reflects a basic mistrust of yourself. If you feel others could cheat or lie to you, you may have a self-judgment that you have lied or been dishonest yourself.

If you have a fear that you might become bored or not know what to do with yourself if you had all the money you needed, imagine creating an exciting life of travel, designing a wonderful work of art, or doing philanthropic work or something else that fascinates you. Sometimes we become addicted to struggle because we don't want to face an even deeper life issue.

If you have a fear that your partner, parents, or siblings will be jealous or feel inferior if you have a lot of money, envision them being happy, proud, and excited for you. If you have difficulty imagining this new picture, look at your beliefs about your partner, parents or siblings. If you hold on to judgmental thoughts about them, you limit your potential for other possible experiences with them. Contrary to popular belief, people can and do change. When you

change your beliefs, your "mirrors" will also change.
Are you willing to see them in a different light?

Step 3

If there are others involved in any of your reasons
for not having what you want, change the subject in
each reason to "I." Here's an example: If you said,
"My friends will think I'm selfish and egotistical,"
change this to "I will think I'm selfish and egotistical."
Or you may have said, "If I had a lot of money, my
spouse might be frightened that I would leave him."
Change this statement to "I might be frightened that I
would leave him." If you said, "Others won't like
me," state why they won't like you. This will enable
you to see the judgment you have about yourself. "I
won't like me because I may become arrogant, selfish,
lazy, or unmotivated."

Step 4

Now change all the "I" statements above to "I
choose to be _____." Instead of saying "I will think
I'm selfish and egotistical," change this to "I choose to
be selfish and egotistical." If you don't see that you
have a choice to be a certain way, you won't know

that you have the power to choose differently. We need to take responsibility for our choices; we need to be accountable for our thoughts, words, and deeds. You may have been helpless or more easily influenced as a child, but you are now capable of being responsible for your own decisions and choices.

Step 5

The statements you have made on these lists should reveal some of the core beliefs you have about yourself or about life. Your list might include such statements as: I choose to be selfish. I choose to be lazy. I choose to be arrogant and mean. I choose to be stupid. I choose to be afraid is not an appropriate statement because "being afraid" is an emotional state, not a character judgment. The kind of person you believe would be afraid would reveal your self-judgment: a weak person, a stupid person, a slow person. In other words, what do you think is wrong with you that would cause you to be fearful?

Now that you are aware of your self-judgments, one way to release them is to accept these judgments and change your perspective toward them. Resisting or trying to hide from them will only give them more power over you. By accepting your self-judgments, you can transform them.

For example, if you have a judgment that you are an obsessive worker, declare that you choose to be obsessive, then convert your judgment into a more positive perspective. Thomas Edison was obsessed. The Wright brothers were obsessed. Albert Einstein was obsessed. One could also say that these people were committed to their ideals and beliefs. You may be in very good company.

A different perspective on the judgment that you are lazy and unmotivated could be that you enjoy life and choose to take it as it comes instead of stressing over it. Another person's perspective of what is valid and valuable in life does not have to be your own perspective. Choose your own beliefs and your own priorities.

Step 6

The following exercise is designed to help you short-circuit your old programming and clear out a self-judgment. You may want to either use a mirror for this next exercise or ask a supportive friend to assist you.

Select one core self-judgment to work on. Facing either the mirror or your friend, look into the eyes of that person across from you and continue to repeat the following statement: "I choose to be _____." Insert the word or phrase that pushes your button, the self-judgment that you dislike. For example, "I choose to be lazy and irresponsible." "I choose to be an arrogant know-it-all." "I choose to be stupid."

Keep saying this phrase until a person's face from your past appears in your memory. The face that appears may be that of a parent, a sibling, a spouse, another relative, or a friend. Once you have a memory of this person saying or implying this remark to you, imagine saying your statement directly to that person. You don't need to remember when this person said this to you, or even whether this person said this to you directly. You only need to sense that this person gave you the impression that there was something wrong with you.

For example, if you remember your father implying or actually accusing you of being lazy and good-for-nothing, imagine looking directly into his eyes and saying, "I choose to be lazy and good-for-nothing." Say it over and over again. For those of you who are resisting this exercise, remember that if you didn't have this judgment about yourself, you wouldn't have a resistance to saying it. If you were asked to say, "I choose to have purple hair," you probably would think it was silly, but you wouldn't have an aversion to saying it.

As you repeat the phrase, "I choose to be _____" over and over again, you may go numb at first, not comprehending what you are saying. This is one of the protective devices you may use to keep from feeling pain. You may also feel anger or sadness as you begin to recall the pain of hearing that unloving comment for the first time. Oftentimes anger is another protective device that we use to cover up hurt feelings.

Keep repeating the phrase until you no longer feel any strong emotion. The hurt and pain will eventually subside as you begin to realize that this comment was not about you at all. It was that person's self-judgment and he or she was so troubled by his or her own inner fear that he or she projected this self-judgment onto you. As a child, you were not aware of this. You took it personally and believed what this person was telling you. Your inner self will begin to see the situation for what it was; your inner self knows the truth about who you really are.

The end result of this exercise will be your ability to release any anger, hurt, or resentment that you may have been carrying deep inside for years. You will instead gain a new understanding, compassion, and forgiveness toward this person. You will not have to force yourself to forgive this person; it will be a natural outcome of your insight and understanding of the situation. After this exercise, that particular self-judgment will no longer hold a charge for you. You will no longer judge yourself or others for having that quality. If you do find yourself being bothered by that word or phrase, you may have to repeat this process until you have released the entire emotional charge.

Going through this process may seem like a great deal of effort, but it's far easier than going through life with self-limiting, self-defeating, self-judgmental thoughts. Moving away from the habit of self-judgment does become easier with time. As you become more aware of your thoughts and beliefs, eventually you won't have any self-judgments to clear. The new habit of self-love and self-awareness will become your way of life.

six

a look at limiting beliefs

In this chapter, let's take a look at some common beliefs that may be limiting you. As you read through the following pages, notice if you agree with any of these beliefs. Write down your own ideas and feelings toward any of the beliefs you agree with, then see if you can view them from a new perspective. Remember, if you insist that you are powerless to change your situation, you won't even begin to see how you can change it. You must realize that you do have the power to make your dreams come true. By letting go of limiting beliefs, you open the door to a whole new world of possibilities.

You can't have your cake and eat it too.

This is scarcity thinking. What good is having a cake if you can't eat it? The basic premise of this belief is that you can't have it all. But you *can* have it all! If you have a cake, of course you can eat it and enjoy it, and then, if you want more cake, you can create another cake. Create an abundance of cake if you want to. Life is not an either-or proposition. You can have your cake and eat it too.

There's not enough . . . .

Many people believe there is not enough love, money, food, water, or other resources for everyone to be happy and fulfilled. This is simply not true. The Source is infinite, and we are unlimited in our ability to create what we need. When we begin to believe and trust that there *is* enough to go around, we will stop suppressing our desires out of fear that there isn't enough. When we begin to see the Universe as totally abundant, we will create abundance instead of scarcity in the world.

When I was in high school, one of my instructors divided the class into groups and told us to pretend that we were different countries. Each group was given a different number of points: Small countries were given fewer points than large countries. The goal of the game was to gain the greatest number of points by persuading other countries to join forces with your country. At the end of the game, the country that had gathered the greatest number of points was the winner.

The coercing, flattering, promising, and lying that went on in this game was astounding. Some groups tried to steal countries away from other groups by offering them a better deal. When the game was over, tempers were high. People accused one another of lying and cheating. The entire class was anxious and tense because each group had wanted to win. The instructor pointed out that this game revealed why we have wars on the planet; he believed this game demonstrated the inherent greedy and manipulative nature of humans.

I wonder what might have happened if the instructor had set a different goal for us? What might have happened if the goal was for each country to have an equal amount of points rather than more points than the others? I believe we would have played an entirely different game. If the goal was to share and make everyone equal and happy, we would have been giving — not just taking. Some of the groups would have to receive points, although receiving can also be difficult for some people.

Many of us have been told that to be happy and fulfilled in life, we need to compete with others and do our best to win. We must win at securing a good job, possessions, wealth, a home, a marriage partner, and so on. We have been taught that there is only so much to go around, that we can lose, that others can take things away from us, or that others can have more than we have which makes us feel "less than" them. Consequently, we compete with one another and fight with one another. We have been taught that we can be victimized and hurt. We don't trust that another person wants us to be happy. We are taught to believe that we could look foolish by giving too much love, so we learn to withhold our love to avoid being hurt or taken advantage of.

Ultimately, all of us want the same things: love, health, happiness, and the fulfillment of our most cherished dreams. If we truly believed in unlimited abundance, and in our ability to create anything and everything we desire through our connection to the Source, we wouldn't live with scarcity thinking. If we truly understood that the love we give is never wasted, but returns to us multiplied, we would choose to help one another achieve our dreams instead of competing with one another.

I am not enough. I am bad.

If you have ever felt depressed, angry, ashamed, or hurt, you have one of these beliefs: "I am not enough" or "I am bad." These limiting beliefs stem from the core belief that we are separate from God. This core belief lies at the root of every problem and every negative experience we have ever had in life. (Chapter Eight offers a shortcut for releasing this limiting belief.) Unfortunately, we suppress our divine, creative power, and hold ourselves back because of these faulty beliefs. The truth is that we are inherently loving beings. While we may not always like how we behave, we are not inherently "bad." We are aspects of God; we are the offspring of God. In the eyes of our Creator, we are perfect and we are always "enough."

It takes a long time.

Time doesn't control your life; you do. If you want to create a better situation in your life, don't wait for time to pass. Change your beliefs, your thoughts, and your actions right now.

For example, if you want a new career, don't wait for time to pass to see if the right job will open up or fall into your hands. Don't wait until you have more time to change your life circumstances. Take the time, make it a priority, and believe in yourself. Decide what you want in a new career, make a plan, and take action. It's not time that must change things, but you that must change them.

If you believe it will take a long time to lose weight, it will take a long time. How much time do you believe it will take? It will probably take that much time. Of course, you may want to take the weight off slowly and give yourself time to adjust emotionally to your new image.

How much time it takes you to attain your goal will depend on how safe you feel in attaining it. If you are afraid to have an intimate relationship, you may be using time as a safety buffer. You might believe that you must accomplish your dreams and goals before you can have a relationship. You may fear that being in a relationship will distract you, slow you down, or pull you off course from achieving your goals. When you change the belief that it is not safe to have a relationship right now, you will open the door to a new relationship.

If you are afraid to live a particular dream right now, honor your need for more time. You may be happy with the belief that your goal will happen "in time" and not mind patiently waiting for it. If you treat time as an advocate, time will act in accordance with your beliefs. If you believe that time is your enemy, then time will be your enemy. If you continue to believe that something is not here yet, then you will always create it "not being here yet." If you believe that love, wealth, good health, or happiness are never here *now*, then you will never experience them being here now. When you start to believe that you can live your dreams right now, you will start to experience them now.

I'm too busy.

Staying too busy is a form of procrastination, which stems, once again, from the fear that we are not enough to have what we want, or that we will be bad if we do have it. Some people stay busy to avoid unpleasant feelings of emptiness, loneliness, or frustration.

Others stay busy because they are afraid to face their dreams and move forward in their lives.

Two women who attended my workshop were using the "I'm too busy" excuse to avoid facing their fear of failure. Each woman wanted to start a business of her own, but when asked why she hadn't done so, each one had an opposite excuse as to why she couldn't live her dream. The first woman commented that she was single, so there was no one to support her and pay her bills if she were to take time off work to try to get a business off the ground. The other woman's excuse was that she was married and would feel guilty and irresponsible if she took time off from her job to start her own business while her husband supported the two of them.

The real issue is that neither woman believes in herself. Neither one really believes she is capable of starting her own business, so each stays too busy at her job to start something new. If each woman believed in herself and made her new business a priority, each would make time for creating a new business.

If you want to make your dreams come true, you must believe it is safe for you to take time to create them. You must be willing to let go of some of the things that keep you so busy. Take a moment to ask yourself these questions: Are you too busy to live your dreams? Who or what are you running away from? Do you believe that other people or outside situations are running your life? Do you need to be busy to feel important? Do you believe you will be a bad parent if you are not driving your children all over town? Do you believe your business will fall apart if you aren't working hard enough? Why are you choosing to stay stuck in your "busy-ness"?

It's someone else's fault.

If you blame others for your problems, you will look to others to solve them for you. If you believe someone else prevents you from being happy, you will think you have to wait for him or her to change before you can be happy. If you believe someone else can stop you from achieving your dreams, you may never attain them.

You may believe that you are destined to be limited by a traumatic childhood. There are many people who have flourished despite their tough beginnings. Why choose to focus on the tough times? What beliefs are you choosing? Do you blame your parents for your current problems? You may be justified in feeling terrible about a difficult past, but this won't create a brighter future. Your parents have passed on their beliefs to you, but you are capable of choosing your own beliefs now.

When you spend time and energy blaming others, you have less time and energy to put into creating a better life for yourself. If you are reacting, you are not creating; you cannot do both at the same time. If you are constantly upset by other people or outer circumstances, you will have little energy left to create what you want in life. Blaming others will never bring you happiness or fulfillment.

God doesn't want me to have what I want.

The ultimate blame is the belief that "God doesn't want me to have what I want." Do you believe God sits on a throne, deciding who should have a life of pain and struggle and who should enjoy a life of ease and luxury? Do you believe there is an evil force that creates a life of pain for some of us while God sits by and judges how we handle it?

God does not judge our creations or our choices; we are the ones who judge them. If you find yourself thinking that God doesn't want you to have something "for your own good," replace the word "God" with "Mom and Dad." When we are little, our parents or other adults deny our wishes and desires "for our own good." We grow up believing that we aren't wise enough or mature enough to make our own decisions. We learn that someone bigger or wiser knows what is good for us; we learn not to trust ourselves. After we outgrow the concept that our parents are infallible god-beings, we replace them with another authority.

You may have prayed and pleaded with God to give you what you want and still you haven't received it. This may explain why you believe God doesn't want you to have what you want. But while you have prayed and pleaded, you may have focused on what you do not have, and aligned yourself with the image of not having it. What you focus on is what you create.

Rather than focusing on the picture of what you don't have, focus on having what you do want. If you choose to be healthy rather than ill, focus on an image of yourself in perfect, radiant health. Affirm that radiant health is yours and feel grateful that your prayers are already answered. A master affirms what she desires just once, then goes about her business, knowing that it is accomplished. By continuing to pray and plead with God, you express feelings of fear and doubt that your desires will manifest.

When you talk to God, affirm that you choose to live your dreams, or simply focus on the image of what you want. If you have created circumstances that are less than pleasing to you, acknowledge that you have created them, affirm your ability to create something new, and choose again. When you declare your commitment to your dreams, you put your energy into choosing, rather than wishing, for them.

Giving too much or doing too much drains my energy.

What will truly drain you is the belief that giving too much or doing too much will deplete your energy. You have access to an infinite supply of energy at all times. If you believe that your energy and resources are limited, if you feel you must conserve these things in order to have more for yourself, you will experience a lack of energy. Some people can go and go all day with excitement and joy for life. At the end of the day, they still have energy. Others struggle to accomplish a few things each day while they sit unhappily behind their desks. At the end of the day, they are worn, tired, and dissatisfied. The difference is not the amount of energy available to them; it is their beliefs and attitudes about life.

A good relationship is hard to find.

Do you believe you have to search and struggle to find a loving relationship? Believing that a good partner is hard to find will only create that experience for you. If you allow for the possibility that you could attract someone easily and effortlessly, your partner could show up at your front door!

One woman I know had a deep desire to be married and have children, but she lived with her mother and worked at home. Her friends constantly teased her, telling her she would never meet someone if she didn't go out and make herself available. This woman strongly believed that she would not have to do anything that wasn't her style. She didn't enjoy going out; she was happy staying at home. She believed in her heart that her mate would show up while she was doing the things she loved to do and living true to herself. Then one day he did show up at her front door. He was the brother of her sister's friend who had come to drop something off for her sister. They were married a short while later and had two beautiful children.

Men and women are bound to have trouble because they are so different.

This belief creates expectations that there will be struggle and unhappiness in our relationships before we even begin. It's not the sex of a person that determines his or her values or behavior, it's his or her beliefs. Contrary to popular belief, not all men have a fear of commitment. Some men deeply desire marriage, while some women strongly desire independence. Some men are great communicators; others fear intimate conversations. Some women express their emotions freely; others have no desire to be openly emotional. We all have the same desire to be loved for who we are. If we think that problems will inevitably arise because men and women are so different and have different needs, then we are destined to always have problems. However, if we can see that problems arise because of our different beliefs, then perhaps we can also see that it's possible to create harmony in our relationships by changing our beliefs.

People don't change.

People do change. You may think people don't change if you hold the same beliefs and perspectives about them. But the problem with this belief is not whether people can change. The problem lies in the belief that someone else *needs* to change. If you have a judgment that someone else needs to change, it's a judgment you have about yourself. Understand that you may need to look inside and change yourself rather than trying to change someone else. When you change the things about yourself that you don't like, you will not be bothered by or even notice other people's shortcomings. When you change, others will often change too. At the very least, you will perceive others differently and they will perceive the changes in you as well.

It is selfish to love myself.

Loving yourself is not selfish at all. The better you feel about yourself, the happier you will be. When you are truly happy and fulfilled, you want everyone else to be happy and fulfilled. That happy and loving energy attracts others who want to be around you and love you, too.

People who do not love themselves are the people who fear no one else will love them either. They then feel they must hoard things, protect themselves, or dominate others. They fear no one else will give or do for them, so they must give and do only for themselves.

Loving yourself does not mean that you will become arrogant and self-serving. The fear of becoming egotistical or appearing arrogant has stopped many people from experiencing their true power and divinity. Rather than judging yourself as bad and holding yourself back out of fear, go ahead and love yourself.

It is truly unselfish to love yourself and be happy because this gives others permission to love themselves and be happy also. People who love and trust themselves are safe to be around. They have little or no judgments, so it is safe for others to open up and be themselves around them. Because they know that they can count on themselves, they have no need to dominate or compete with others.

If I am happy and successful, others won't love me.

People are often afraid that if they are happy, prosperous, and successful, other people will be envious and resentful and withdraw their love. Others have a fear that if they are happy and prosperous, they will be hurting those they love by making them feel inferior or worthless.

If you are happy and successful, this doesn't mean that others will dislike you. Many people are awed and inspired by happy and successful people. Notice how many people love to be around successful celebrities.

The limitations we put on ourselves because we fear being unloved is amazing. Many people would love to work less and make more money, but would feel guilty if this were to happen. They are afraid that others would be jealous and not love them anymore. All too often, we sacrifice our own happiness and hold ourselves back by staying in "the pit" with everyone else. We believe this is the most loving, compassionate thing we can do for others. We may even find ourselves trying to rescue everyone else by helping them out of the pit first.

Unfortunately, others have the same fear of being unloved or considered selfish if they get out of the pit first. Consequently, everyone stays safely down in the pit, struggling and suffering together. The belief that you must sacrifice in order to be lovable or loving is a limiting belief that does not empower anyone. It only teaches others that they, too, must make sacrifices in order to prove they are worthy of love. A better approach is to have the courage to get out of the pit first. Risk facing envy, rejection, and judgments from others so that you can help them out of the pit by leading the way.

One single mother by the name of Rhonda worked very hard for years to support herself and her daughter. Rhonda was constantly making sacrifices for the welfare of her daughter, and she was often tired and worn out as a result of all her efforts. Rhonda didn't realize that she was teaching her daughter how to sacrifice also. She learned one day that her daughter was considering not going to college because she felt guilty leaving her mother after all the sacrifices that had been made for her. The daughter was afraid that her mother would be all alone and unhappy without her. She also loved her mother and wanted to honor her by being just like her.

When Rhonda realized how her own behavior had affected her daughter, she decided to change her life. She realized that unless she began to live a happy and fulfilling life herself, her daughter would never feel free to live her own dreams. They would both end up sacrificing their dreams and struggling through life.

Instead of falling into the old habit of the sacrificing mother, Rhonda began to live her life more fully. In doing so, she inspired her daughter to follow her own dreams.

Love others enough to lead the way. Create love, abundance, joy, health, and fulfillment in your life to show others that it's possible. Successful people can inspire others to see that they, too, can break free from ordinary boundaries and experience the fulfillment of their dreams.

My thoughts and feelings have no effect on the health of my body.

We know that our thoughts and emotional states do affect our physical health. Western medicine has linked stress with high blood pressure, migraine headaches, heart attacks, and other physical ailments. More heart attacks occur at 9:00 A.M. on Monday morning than at any other time. Mental fatigue, emotional stress, job dissatisfaction, and general unhappiness all contribute to health problems.

While working with clients who had cancer, AIDS, and other potentially life-threatening illnesses, I discovered that all of them had deep-seated, unresolved guilt or anger from the past which had been eating them up inside. Each one remembered at one time having a feeling that he or she shouldn't be alive, a feeling that he or she didn't deserve to be alive, or an actual death wish. Some of these people had experienced these feelings for many years.

I believe that one of the reasons we are experiencing a dramatic increase in diseases such as cancer and AIDS is due to the incredible amount of attention that is focused on them. Everywhere you turn, people are talking about cancer and AIDS. The fear of these diseases has captured our attention and permeated our consciousness. Whatever we focus our energy upon will increase. If we truly want to rid the world of these diseases, we need to stop giving them power and energy by focusing our attention on them. We must focus on the solution, not the problem. It's not the people who hate disease who will end disease. It's the people who focus on health and well-being who will dissipate the fear around these diseases and, therefore, lessen their impact on humanity.

Many illnesses stem from mental and emotional causes. Physical problems often begin with a mental and emotional dilemma that wasn't dealt with or solved on the mental or emotional level. A physical ill-ness is your body's way of letting you know that something is wrong with your inner beliefs and emo-tions. If you believe that certain foods will make you ill and you stop eating those foods, your inner self will find another way to get your attention. There are people who can only eat a few things because they continue to believe that certain foods are the cause of their problem instead of looking at the mental and emotional causes.

It doesn't matter what type of health practitioner you go to. What matters is that you *believe* you can and will be healed. Your beliefs have a profound effect on your body. If you are overweight, you may have unconsciously created extra layers for protection or because you think others will feel less threatened by you. You may believe it is natural to gain weight as you grow older, or that a lack of exercise will cause you to gain weight. You may believe that you inher-ited the tendency to gain weight, or that you will look like your parents. Your body will conform to your beliefs and the mental image that you hold in your mind. To change your body or your health, you must change your beliefs.

When you experience an illness or a pain in your body, focus your attention on the area of your body where you are experiencing discomfort and ask your body what it wants to say to you. Ask your body what it needs, then act on that answer to heal your situation.

After learning about this technique, a man named David, who attended a class that I was teaching, shared his experience. For months David had experienced chronic back pain. When he placed his hands on the painful area in his back and asked his back to tell him what it wanted to say to him, he got a mental picture of his father. His father's face appeared to be anxious and troubled. Within moments, David realized what thoughts and energy he had been storing in his back.

A few months earlier, shortly before his back problems began, David was informed that he would receive a job promotion and a pay raise. He realized that he felt guilty about his advancement because for the first time in his life, he was about to surpass his father's lifetime accomplishments. His father, whom he loved very much, had worked very hard to support his family, but had never made much money. David was afraid that his success would make his father feel inferior. Because he felt guilty, he was afraid to move forward with his life, and this created the tension in his back.

When David asked for the solution to his dilemma, his inner voice explained that his father would actually be proud of his son. In addition, to resolve his guilt, David was to go to his father and thank him for all of his support and guidance through the years. He realized that if his father felt partially responsible for his son's success, rather than feeling inferior, his father might feel a sense of accomplishment. His father might be happy that all of his hard work had been worth something. David followed the advice of his inner voice and within days, his back pain was gone.

I have to work hard to make more money.

Some people believe the harder they work, the more money they will make, but there is little evidence that this belief is true. Ditch diggers and coal miners work much harder than people who sit at desks in air-conditioned offices and talk on the phone all day. And yet, the people at the desks usually make more money. There are many hard-working people who don't always succeed in attaining their dreams. All too often they end up stressed, frustrated, unhealthy, broke, and disillusioned. Working harder is no guarantee that you will make more money.

One woman I know was working between sixty and one hundred hours a week at her job. She made a modest salary working at a performing arts theater during the day, in the evenings, and on almost every weekend when there were performances. When she quit her job and started her own business, she chose to work less than twenty hours a week and yet she made more than three times her previous salary. This woman had changed her belief that she had to work hard to make money.

Money is the root of all evil.

Money was created to serve us, to simplify life, to help us interact and trade services with one another without having to drag livestock or other products around with us. Many people speak of money as the root of all evil. Money isn't evil; money is just coins and paper. Sometimes people have abused others for money because of their limited and faulty beliefs. These people may believe there isn't enough money or that they must hurt others to have money.

If you make money an enemy or consider it evil, don't be surprised if making money is difficult for you. If you believe that money will only bring you misery, you may not allow yourself to have much money. You must make friends with money; appreciate it, acknowledge it, and sincerely love it. Everything responds to love, including money.

A friend of mine named Michelle was constantly complaining how much she disliked money. Michelle believed that money was the cause of all her problems. Of course, she never had any money. After we discussed the idea that she wouldn't attract money if she despised it, she decided to make friends with money. Michelle loves dolphins, so she decided to imagine money as tiny little dolphins that would come to play with her. She had so much fun imagining money in the form of dolphins that she began to feel friendly toward money. Soon, money was not a problem for her. Michelle now has a renewed respect for money and enjoys having it.

Money won't buy you happiness.

This may be one of those beliefs that was handed down to us to pacify us and make us think that we can't have or shouldn't have everything we want. There are plenty of people who are very happy having an abundance of money to spend as they choose. Money does buy you happiness if you believe it does. Of course, money is not the source of your happiness, but nothing outside of you is the source of your happiness — or your anger, or your sadness. You choose to believe what will make you happy. Money can make you happy or unhappy; it's your choice, your belief.

If you believe having an abundance of money will make you happy, then having an abundance of money will bring you happiness. However, if you have a deep belief that nothing will ever make you happy and that life never works out for you, then not even money will make you happy.

My job is the source of my abundance and security.

Your job is not the source of your abundance. Nothing outside of you is your source. Infinite Intelligence is your Source, and because you are connected to this Source at all times, all things are possible and available to you.

Your job is not the source of your security. The only real security we have is believing and trusting in ourself and in our connection to the Source. Whenever we believe that our source comes from outside of us, we live in fear and insecurity that the source could disappear.

If we see that money and other forms of abundance can come from anywhere, even unexpected places, then we will not limit the possibilities. To change your concepts and expand your possibilities of where money can come from, imagine that money can come to you, no matter what you do with your time. Visualize money coming to you from unexpected places; imagine that it is flowing to you and falling all around you. Imagine holding it in your hands, or generously giving it to others. Know that you have total access to this money; it is being created just for you. You don't need to take it away from others or work hard for it. After doing this exercise, you may begin to notice many different ways that money, or abundance in other forms, comes to you.

One couple I know spent five minutes every night visualizing money floating down from the sky. One day, out of the blue, they received a call from a game show inviting the wife to be a guest on their show. The wife loved game shows, but she had not planned anything or taken any steps to be on the show. Through coincidence and synchronicity, she received the invitation and won $25,000 while she was on the show.

It may seem that working hard or struggling for money is the only way that it can come to you. Believing that money can magically appear may seem entirely impossible. But remember, our perception of reality has been limited. Our beliefs about money are learned; we have been conditioned to believe in struggle and hard work.

Why not consider other possibilities? Imagine yourself doing what you love to do. Then imagine money easily coming to you.

What beliefs might keep you from easily receiving money? Would you feel guilty? Are you afraid that you would be judged as lazy and unproductive? Do you believe that only lucky people don't have to work for their money? Why aren't you lucky?

We have learned to believe that money comes from working, and that if we don't work, we won't make money. But there are people who have money who don't work at all. There are people who work and still have no money to show for it. There are people who inherit money, people who win money, and people who make money from investments. There are numerous ways that money or other forms of abundance can come to you. But first, let go of the limiting belief that money can only come from your job or by working for it.

part four

Creating with New Beliefs

"To fly as fast as thought, to anywhere that is, you must begin by knowing that you have already arrived."

—RICHARD BACH, *Jonathan Livingston Seagull*

seven

living the life of your dreams

Now that you have learned how to change or release your limiting beliefs, here are some simple steps you can take to create the life of your dreams.

The Power of Love

One of the most profound ways to create what you want is to use the power of love. Loving energy always attracts what we want in life. If you want a healthy or attractive body, love your body. Appreciate that it has been serving you. Acknowledge that it has cooperated with your inner pictures and taken a safe form for you.

Nurture your body and be kind to it. Pamper and comfort your body, and it will reflect that loving kindness.

If you want a new career, make sure that you love that career. Imagine the love you feel for the process of writing, or painting, or publishing, or counseling, or teaching, or engineering, or working on computers, or learning the stock market. Feel warmth, passion, and excitement for what you want to be doing.

If you want a loving relationship in your life, love yourself as well as others. Feel love and compassion toward everyone. If you radiate love, you will attract love to you. I like to use the following analogy to help people create their own consciousness of love: If you wanted to experience the beauty and magic of Hawaii, you would travel to the State of Hawaii. Once in Hawaii, you could experience everything the state had to offer: tropical breezes; warm, clear water; delicious fruits; interesting cultural events; the aloha spirit of the local people; Hawaiian music; and so on.

If you want to experience what love has to offer, move to the State of Love. What do you imagine the natives in the State of Love would be like? How would you feel about your surroundings in this state? What qualities would you experience in yourself if you were living in the State of Love? Would you feel generous and giving? Would you be patient and understanding? Would you be trusting and forgiving? Would you see others as perfect in their own ways? Move to the State of Love, and experience everything that love has to offer.

Follow in Your Own Footsteps

Another simple way to create what you want is to follow the same steps that you took when you were successful in another area of your life. What have you created that you are truly pleased with? How did you do it? To discover the beliefs that work for you, ask yourself these questions: How did you bring that object, person, or event into your life? Write down what thoughts, feelings, and expectations you had, and what actions you took.

Now, think of something you want in your life right now. Are you doing the same kind of things that you did before? Are you having similar thoughts, or taking similar actions that you took when you were successful?

One man who attended a workshop of mine told me how happy he was that he had a new car. When I asked him how he got it, he said he first decided that it was time to buy a new car, then he made a list of what was important to him in a car. He decided on the qualities of comfort, economy, appearance, endurance, and performance. Then he did research to find what type of car was rated high in those categories. He worked out a budget, looked at a variety of cars, and chose the car that met his standards.

When I asked him what he would like to have that he didn't now have, his answer was a new career. Then I asked him if he had taken similar steps to acquire a new career. No, he had not. He hadn't even decided that it was time to look for a new career. Deciding it was time to buy a new car was the first step he had taken before. No wonder he didn't have a new career. If this man takes steps to create a new career similar to those he took to find a new car, he will have a new career. Obviously these steps work for him, because he used them to obtain a new car.

A friend of mine had created a very successful and profitable business. She was pleased with her accomplishments, but now she wanted to create a loving relationship. The steps she had used to create her dream business included deciding what she loved to do. She decided that the excitement and potential rewards involved in having her own business were greater than the risks. She really *believed* she could succeed. She overcame every obstacle and fear that arose by remaining focused and committed to her dream. She didn't quit until she achieved her goals.

When I asked her if she had taken the same steps to create a relationship in her life, she replied that she had taken none of the same steps. She had thought about being in a relationship, but she had not committed to creating a relationship the same way that she had committed to her other goals. She admitted that she didn't believe it was possible for her to have a relationship while she was establishing her business. It was no surprise to me that she didn't have a relationship yet.

Write down the steps you took to successfully accomplish one of your goals. Notice if you are taking the same kind of actions to acquire something else you want. This may not be the only way to achieve your goals, but obviously your belief in these steps works for you.

Focus on the Solution

To create what you want using your new beliefs, focus on the solution rather than on the problem. If you focus on the problem, you only create more of the problem and reinforce the belief that there is a problem. If you focus on the solution, you reinforce your belief that there is a solution and begin to see solutions.

Let's use sports as an example of focusing our attention on the goal. If a golfer wants to hit his golf ball into a hole on the green, he focuses his attention on where he wants the ball to go rather than on the places he fears the ball may go. When he visualizes the ball going into the hole, his mind sends messages to his body, which in turn makes subtle adjustments aimed at helping him achieve that goal. If the golfer were to focus his attention on what he fears may happen, if he imagines the ball going into a sand trap rather than into the hole, there is a greater probability that the ball will indeed go off course. When you focus your attention on your goal, your mental, emotional, and physical energies support that goal and work toward creating the result you want.

Ask and You Shall Receive

This statement has been taught by many of the world's spiritual masters. The promise is simple: Ask and you shall receive. There are no strings attached. There are no conditions such as, "If you deserve it" or "If it's for your highest good" or "If it's the right time." Ask and you shall receive. All you need to do is believe that it is true, and "As you believe, so shall it be done unto you."

Speak Your Word

"In the beginning was the Word." God created by using the word; the word has creative power. Speak your word, and call what you want into existence. Then trust that what you have spoken is being created now. Believe that God has no judgments about what you want to create in your life. As long as you do not limit yourself by believing that you are bad or not enough, you will see that you are always connected to the Source and have the ability to create whatever you want.

Trust

Trust comes from believing and knowing that what you want is yours. Trust is not blind hope; it is based on an inner knowing. When you choose a goal and have a clear intention to achieve your goal, trust that your inner self and Infinite Intelligence are helping you to achieve it.

When a desire arises within you, trust that desire. Also trust your impulses to act on your desire, because this is one way that your inner self communicates with you. Your impulses will spontaneously move you in the direction of your dreams; Infinite Intelligence will manage the details and create the event more magically and with less effort than you could possibly do on your own.

Imagine that you have decided to travel to a foreign country. You decide on a destination, set your intentions to achieve the goal, and book a flight. As the plane races down the runway, you are aware of the forward movement. You can feel the momentum of the plane. You can feel the pressure on your body. These are obvious signs that you are in motion. Similarly, once you select a goal and begin to take action to accomplish that goal, you can sense movement. You know something is happening because you can see changes.

However, once you are in the air, you no longer have the same sensation that you are moving. You are moving faster in the air than you were on the ground, but you don't feel any movement at all. It is at this point, when it feels like nothing is happening, that most of us panic and think we must do something to move forward again. Instead of trusting that every-thing is in process and our desire is on its way, we start to pace the aisles of the plane, thinking this will help us to arrive at our destination more quickly. As we walk toward the front of the plane, we may feel we are in control once again and making progress, but then we have to turn around and walk toward the back of the plane. Now it seems that all the progress we have made is falling apart; we are losing ground and moving backward. In reality, the plane is still moving us for-ward toward our destination.

Your vision and intention set the process in motion, and Infinite Intelligence goes about creating your desires. If, out of fear, you panic and doubt that your desire is manifesting for you, you hinder the process. If you turn your thoughts to the old picture, your inner self will once again create the old picture.

Sometimes what you need to do is sit down, relax, and be still inside, while trusting that the Universe will take you to your destination. Let the magic happen. Keep your doubts and fears out of the way. The quieter and more trusting you are on your journey, the easier it is for you to hear your inner voice, the voice that will guide you about what to do next.

With trust, the steps required to create your dreams are simple. Trust that your desires are valid; it's okay for you to live your dreams. Trust your inner voice and intuition; they will tell you what steps to take. Trust that what you desire is being manifested for you now. Trust that even if it looks like nothing is happening, your intentions have set the process in motion, and Infinite Intelligence is taking care of the details.

Stay in the Moment

Staying in the present moment is an important step in creating what you want. Our point of power is in the present moment. If our energy is always focused on the past or worried about the future, we will not have the energy to accomplish anything in the present. It's important to look to the future, to envision a goal and to see what direction to head, but then we must stay focused in the present and allow our intuition to tell us what actions to take.

One way to keep your energy focused in the present is to focus on your breath. When you focus on your breath, you no longer feel stressed or worried about the past or the future. It is a simple reminder to help you stay in the present moment.

Imagine that you are in a sailboat on the ocean. In the distance you spot the island you wish to sail to, but as you proceed on your journey, you also stay present and alert to your immediate surroundings. You pay attention to your boat, your sails, your rudder, and the ocean directly in front of you. If there are any rocks or obstacles in your way, you want to be able to spot them. While keeping your vision on your goal, you stay in the present moment, and appreciate the journey. This is one of the best ways to reach your dreams without struggle.

Pray

Prayer is a wonderful way to recognize, remember, and reconnect with the divine power. Prayer does not necessarily mean that you beg or plead for what you want. Begging and pleading are based on fear and only reinforce the belief that you do not already have what you want. Universal Intelligence already knows what you desire in your heart. When you fear or doubt that what you want is manifesting for you, you get in your own way — you stop the process from happening easily and effortlessly. If you have faith, if you know, if you really believe, you can move mountains.

Prayer can be used for affirmation and gratitude, knowing that what you are praying for already exists. "Not my will, but thy will" was not meant to indicate that there is opposition between your will and God's will, but to remind you that there is only one will: God's will. Your will is not separate from God's will. If you have a desire for something, it is God's desire. There are no desires other than what God desires. There is no will other than God's will. It is true that we have free will and that we can create anything we choose, but it is still God's will. Our will and our desires are not separate from God's will and desires because we are not separate from God. Our desires come from God.

How will you know if you no longer have any limiting beliefs preventing you from having what you desire? How will you know if you are really loving yourself and believing in your dreams? It's simple. All of your dreams will come true.

eight

the shortcut to happiness
and fulfillment

The core belief that is the source of all of our problems and unhappiness is the belief that we are separate: separate from God, separate from one another, separate from our inner Self, and separate from whatever we wish to create. As long as we believe we are separate from God, our Source, we will never know the great creative power that is ours. We will not know that we are aligned with God and have access to all of God's kingdom, to anything we desire, at all times.

If we look at God as Universal Intelligence, as omnipresent, omniscient, and omnipotent, we will see that it is impossible to be separate from God. Omni means the ultimate all or all-inclusive. Omnipresent means present everywhere. We cannot be separate from God; God is as close as our breath. Omniscient means all-knowing. Being connected to God, we also have access to all knowledge. Omnipotent means all-powerful, the only power there is. If God is all power, there cannot be a separate power, especially one that opposes God.

A drop of water is not all of the water in the ocean, but it is water nonetheless, and it has all the properties that make up water. A ray of light is not all the light there is, but it is light nonetheless. We are God-beings. We are not all of what is God, but we are aspects of God, or images of God nonetheless. And, if we are aspects of God, if we are connected to God we, too, must have the same creative powers and attributes that God has. To believe that we are separate from God or not as good as God, is simply an illusion created by faulty beliefs. It is impossible to be disconnected from our Source because the Source is present everywhere. Where could we be that God is not?

We began believing that we were separate from God when we began believing in good and evil. Since

God is good and we believe we are not always good, then we believe we are not what God is. But we can only believe in an evil or "dark side" to us if we believe that light comes from a source outside of us. When the source of light shines on a "separate" object, a shadow is cast on the far side of the object, causing the appearance of a dark side. However, when the source of light comes from within, there can be no dark side. What is the dark side of the sun? God is within us and around us. Within us is the source of light; we have no dark side except in our imagination. If we stop judging ourselves and others as "not good" or "not what God is," then we might remember our true divinity and unleash the creative power that is truly God within us.

God is a Creator. We are created in God's image, and we also create. We create our own experience of life, our own "life drama," but we have forgotten this. We become so attached to the illusion of our drama that we forget we are its creators. When we are in the dream state, everything in our dream seems real to us. We don't know that we are dreaming until we wake up. But the same can be said about the waking state of consciousness. While we are awake, everything seems real to us. We experience each state of consciousness as the only reality there is while we are in it. It is not until we move from the dream state to the waking state that our dreams are revealed or seen as an illusion. What will be revealed to us about the waking state when we move to another state of consciousness?

The only thing that is real, the only thing that remains with us when we achieve a heightened state of awareness, is the presence of God. All else is a temporary illusion of the mind. We use the mind to experience the act of creating. We create, and we perceive our creations. But we have forgotten who we really are. We have forgotten that we are creators — that our thoughts and feelings have the power to create. For far too long, we have believed that we are lesser beings than we really are. We have believed that we are less than truly powerful, loving, magnificent, and magical beings.

We are now in the process of redefining what it means to be human. I believe that we are in the process of awakening and remembering our divinity. We are learning to be conscious, aware creators. The best way to discard any beliefs that limit us is to remember who we really are. This is the shortcut to happiness and fulfillment.

Many spiritual masters have attempted to remind us of our divinity. One master, whom we know as Jesus, reminded us of our true nature. Jesus said, "He who has seen me, has seen the Father." He said he was the son of God and that we were his brethren, which makes us the children of God also. He claimed that the wondrous works he had done, we would do also. He saw through the illusions of illness, blindness, and lameness; he saw the true divine nature of wholeness and perfection in everyone. His understanding of the truth behind the veil of illusion helped others to dissolve their illusions and to be healed instantly.

Jesus also showed us that death is an illusion that has no power over us. He proved that we are made of light by transforming himself into light before many witnesses. But instead of believing that Christ came to remind us of who we really are, people thought that only Christ was God. Christ did not say, "Worship me." He said, "Follow me, I can teach you the truth about life. I will show you the way. You can do what I do."

Christ came to free us from our fears, to free us from believing in the nightmares we had created. Christ came to "save" us from ourselves, from being stuck in the pain of our own illusions. He didn't teach dogma; he demonstrated divinity. He showed by example that true divinity is loving, compassionate, nonjudgmental, powerful, and magical. The limiting judgments, rules, and dogmas that we impose upon ourselves keep us from realizing our divinity.

As long as we are alive, we might as well enjoy our lives. Why not create what we choose to experience and enjoy our creations? Why not become conscious creators in our waking state? We struggle with life when we forget that we have the power to create our lives as we please. By quieting the chatter in our minds, we can hear the inner Self that knows who we really are, that knows of our greater power and of our connection to Source.

If we want to create a new life, we can do it at any time. If we have a desire for a new experience, it's all right to trust that desire. We don't need to judge it. Desire is the beginning of all creation. Desire is Universal Intelligence choosing what to create next; it is simply an aspect of God desiring to have that experience. We inherently desire to create, experience, and expand our potential. But we limit our natural impulses and the impulses of all life to grow and expand by telling ourselves that things are not possible, safe, or wise to do. Since everything is ultimately God or Source, why would we limit or judge God?

Planet Earth is not a place of punishment or a place that we must tolerate until we can reap our rewards in a better place. Being human is not a low form of existence that we must somehow escape; nor do we need to struggle to "go home" to the Source. We were never separated from the Source, except in our imaginations; we have always been united with God.

When we acknowledge our connection with God, the Source of all creation, life can become a beautiful playground. Life can become lighter, easier, and more fun. When we remember who we are, when we have dominion over our thoughts and beliefs, we become conscious creators. We simply enjoy the experience of creating, knowing that the only true reality is God, our Source and Creator, who loves and creates.

Proof of God's presence & abundance

- black MR2
- trip to Greece
- trip to Austin?
- house next door to Olia

about the author

Pamala Oslie is a renowned psychic counselor and the author of *Life Colors: What Your Aura Colors Say About You*. As a psychic counselor, she identifies the personality patterns revealed in the aura and the underlying beliefs that keep us from living our true potential. Pamala is a frequent and popular guest on many radio and television shows, and gives workshops and seminars throughout the country on auras, psychic and intuitive development, and the power of beliefs. She lives in Santa Barbara, California.

To contact the author, please write:

Pamala Oslie
Post Office Box 30035
Santa Barbara, California 93130

(805) 687-6604
http://www.auracolors.com

How Did I Do It?

1. Made a decision
2. Lived it each day
3. Planned for it the night before, week of, etc.
4. Became my identity, "who I was."
5. Enjoyed the process
6. Talked @ it to others
7. Believed there was no other option.
8. Not swayed by what others were doing
9. Believed I _would_, not that I could.
10. Proud of each baby step
11. Had a goal
    - MARATHON = running
    - ORANGE OUTFIT = weight
    - TENNECO SCHOLARSHIP = kids succeed
12. Overcame obstacles by wanting GOAL more than this temporary treat.
    - RUNNING IN RAIN or AT NIGHT
    - NOT EATING AT BANQUETS, etc.

Also from Amber-Allen Publishing

The Seven Spiritual Laws of Success by Deepak Chopra

Creating Affluence by Deepak Chopra

Child of the Dawn by Gautama Chopra

The Four Agreements by don Miguel Ruiz

The Angel Experience by Terry Lynn Taylor

The Legend of Tommy Morris by Anne Kinsman Fisher

Seth Speaks (A Seth Book) by Jane Roberts

The Nature of Personal Reality (A Seth Book) by Jane Roberts

The Magical Approach (A Seth Book) by Jane Roberts

The Oversoul Seven Trilogy by Jane Roberts

Individual and the Nature of Mass Events (A Seth Book)
by Jane Roberts

The Way Toward Health (A Seth Book) by Jane Roberts

The "Unknown" Reality (A Seth Book) by Janc Roberts

Dreams, "Evolution," and Value Fulfillment (A Seth Book)
by Jane Roberts

The 12 Stages of Healing by Donald Epstein, D.C.
with Nathaniel Altman

Audio

The Seven Spiritual Laws of Success by Deepak Chopra

The Crescent Moon by Deepak Chopra

Living Without Limits by Deepak Chopra & Wayne Dyer

Living Beyond Miracles by Deepak Chopra & Wayne Dyer

Return of the Rishi by Deepak Chopra

Escaping the Prison of the Intellect by Deepak Chopra

Sacred Verses, Healing Sounds (Vol I & II) by Deepak Chopra

Available at Bookstores Everywhere
or call toll-free (800) 624-8855

Amber-Allen Publishing is dedicated to bringing
a message of love and inspiration to all who seek
a higher purpose and meaning in life.

For a catalog of our books and cassettes, please contact:

Amber-Allen Publishing
Post Office Box 6657
San Rafael, California 94903

(415) 499-4657 (phone)
(415) 499-3174 (fax)

Email: amberallen@infoasis.com
Visit our website: http://www.amberallen.com